ISLAMIC PERSPECTIVES ON Prayers & Coping with Sickness

WHAT EVERYONE'S SAYING...

I have just read *Islamic Perspectives on Prayers & Coping with Sickness* and I am struck by the thoughtfulness, *taqwa* (God-consciousness) and care that emanate from this book. It is a handy source for Muslims and non-Muslims alike. Mr Syed speaks out of his personal experience as a visitor to sick and hospitalized Muslims. This handbook offers simple, God-fearing advice to the many dilemmas facing the Muslim patient. It offers poignant advice on prayer, fasting and cleanliness, just to mention a few of the topics.

The references are quite adequate for doing further research about the topics covered in the book and it includes specific prayers for various times of illness and death.

As a chaplain working in institutional settings, I am quite impressed by the advice given to those people who visit Muslim patients. This advice is well rounded and quite instructive. If the visitors would take this information with them when making their visit, the visited person would definitely encounter someone who is sensitive, caring and informed. The visitor would be comfortable during the visit, ask appropriate questions and know what to do, and what not to do. This combination is a key to good hospital visiting and creates an atmosphere where healing can occur.

I am delighted by the dedication Mr Syed has placed in this work. It is a great resource for the health care team, the Muslim visitor and the patient. Brother Amjad, may Allah reward you for this worthy effort in taking care of the sick and hospitalized.

Chaplain M. AbdurRashid Taylor, Director, Islamic Chaplaincy Services, Canada,
and Supervisor, Spiritual and Religious Care Services,
Centre for Addiction and Mental Health

$$\text{C3} \bigcirc \text{80}$$

Books on patient care and coping with sickness are rare indeed. I find *Islamic Perspectives on Prayers & Coping with Sickness* very comprehensive and practical. It will be a boon to Muslims in every corner of the globe. Brother Amjad's book reflects the true spirit of Islam and I recommend it most highly.

Sheik Ibrahim Malabari

$$\text{C3} \bigcirc \text{80}$$

It is very important for a patient to be continuously in touch with God, especially under the agony of sickness. In this truly invaluable guidebook, Amjad Syed has made life easy for Muslim patients to cope with sickness through faith in the healing power of prayers.

Dr Diane Bridges, D.Min.,
Director, Spiritual Care, Trillium Health Centre

There's no real shortage of books on *ibadaat* (prayers). What was really needed was a work to guide the lay Muslim to uphold the prayer habit under difficult and trying situations…. Brother Amjad Syed must be congratulated for a job well done, for his highly readable *Islamic Perspectives on Prayers & Coping with Sickness* has surpassed all my expectations.

Mirza Shafi, Muslim Social Worker in hospitals and jails

ೞ ○ ೞ

I have gone through pain and suffering and know the value of health. I was bedridden in hospital while undergoing heart surgery when I read through the draft copy of this wonderful work. There were innumerable disabilities to conduct my *ibadaat* with utter peace of mind but my discussions with Amjad and a reading of his book made me more confident in my *ibadaat*. I would certainly recommend that everyone — all the healthy and the sick – make good use of this knowledge.

Dr Afzalunnisa Syeda, author's sister

ೞ ○ ೞ

I am glad to see this book and wish as many Muslims as possible will read *Islamic Perspectives on Coping with Sickness* before they really need to conduct prayers in sickness. It is time Muslims realize that *salaat* can be conducted in a hospital bed and that a hat is not an essential part of the outfit for it.

Dr Ibrahim Syed, Scientist

ೞ ○ ೞ

Thanks to Brother Amjad Syed for his compilation of this useful book, showing how easy and simple it is to remain steadfast in Islam under all kinds of conditions, in coping with sickness or in conducting routine prayers, with all confidence, for oneself or for those who are too disabled to pray for themselves. I recommend this excellent handbook to all Muslims. Read it before it's too late.

Imam Nadjad Hafizowich, Bosnian Islamic Centre

ISLAMIC PERSPECTIVES ON Prayers & Coping with Sickness

Written and compiled by
AMJAD R. M. SYED

Canada

Copyright © 2002 by Amjad R. M. Syed

ISLAMIC PERSPECTIVES ON PRAYERS
& COPING WITH SICKNESS
ISBN 0-9731641-0-7

Published by
ISNA Canada Headquarters
Islamic Society of North America
2200 South Sheridan Way
Mississauga, Ontario L5J 2M4
Tel (905) 403-8406
Fax (905) 403-8409
Email: isna@isnacanada.com
Website: www.isnacanada.com

Edited and designed by Rashid Mughal
Cover art by Salimah Ribeiro-Dewji

Printed and bound in Canada

وَنُنَزِّلُ مِنَ الْقُرْآنِ
مَا هُوَ شِفَاءٌ وَرَحْمَةٌ لِّلْمُؤْمِنِينَ

We send down
in the Qur'an
that which is a healing
and a mercy to those
who believe

Qur'an 17:82

وَإِذَا مَرِضْتُ فَهُوَ يَشْفِينِ

When
I am ill,
it is He
who cures me

Qur'an 26:80

Contents

FOREWORD

IN its opening lines the Holy Qur'an tells us: *Praise be to Allah, the Cherisher and Sustainer of the Worlds; Most Gracious, Most Merciful: Master of the Day of Judgment. You alone we worship; You alone we ask for help. Guide us to the straight path; the path of those whom You favored, not the path of those who earn Your anger, nor of those who go astray.*

The Qur'an also tells us that Prophet Muhammad (Peace and blessings of Allah be upon him) demonstrated exceptional strength of character and nobility of conduct in every kind of situation. Muslims therefore aspire to imitate the Prophet's conduct and to learn the sayings that demonstrate he not only uttered gems of wisdom but also practised what he preached. (Surah 68:4)

The Prophet taught us by his supreme example how we may uplift ourselves during difficult times, modify our conduct and behavior, and improve our religious and worldly affairs.

For more than a thousand years now, Muslim scholars and jurists have produced countless books, monographs and texts on a variety of subjects related to Islam. Equally enormous is the output of Islamic literature in English in recent years.

However, it is ironic that many libraries – whether we look to the East or West – are not adequately equipped to guide the average Muslim on day-to-day spiritual issues and temporal matters such as sickness, stillbirth or death.

In this regard, Brother Amjad Syed has done a marvelous job to fill such a vacuum wherever it exists. The topics and issues discussed in *Islamic Perspectives on Prayers & Coping with Sickness* are contemporary and relevant. They are meant to inform, educate, and inspire every Muslim to cope with helplessness and hopelessness, whether in sickness or in health.

The author — a 30-year veteran hospital worker, caregiver and an advisory committee member of two hospitals — makes prudent use of his scientific training in handling the subjects with meticulous care. He identifies and delineates precisely what is important about the issues, traces the sources, authenticates the statements and focuses on what is essential and practical, using scientific research methodology.

His scholarship is precise and his treatment concise.

Islamic Perspectives on Prayers & Coping with Sickness is a unique sourcebook for people to practice *ibadaat* and to cope correctly with sickness, their own or that of a family member or friend.

This book is destined to become an invaluable source of comfort for specialists and patients alike, and for volunteer caregivers and hospital staff everywhere. Finally, for those who wish to make a detailed and comprehensive study, the book is a veritable springboard into the great ocean of Islamic literature on these issues.

Hany K. A. Ali, Ph.D., P.Eng.

PREFACE

THE idea for *Islamic Perspectives on Prayers & Coping with Sickness* came from my own experience, study and observation of various *ibadaat* practices by the patients.

Sometimes, perhaps out of ignorance, some Muslims are more concerned about local customs than their *faraiz* (obligations). For example, they may shy off from performing *wudu* in public washrooms, although people in the West have come to recognize the importance of hand washing and *wudu*. Perhaps *tahara* will come next in the West!

Some Muslims feel uncomfortable to perform *salaat* in a public place even though many non-Muslims approve of it and see nothing wrong with it.

A well-read, older Muslim who performed his daily *salaat* regularly, stopped it on account of being hospitalized. Upon enquiring, he answered, "This is not a clean place for *salaat*. I have difficulty in *tahara*, my bed is not so clean, and the medical staff keeps walking around. *Insha Allah*, when I get home, I'll perform all the missed *salawaat*."

Unfortunately, he never made it home. May Allah forgive him.

Many Muslims today appear to attach great importance to customs and even *bida* and *shirk* than to the teachings of the Qur'an and the traditions of our dear Prophet (PBUH). It is therefore incumbent upon every knowledgeable Muslim to assume the task of re-educating those who may have strayed from their obligations.

The upkeep of *salawaat* is the key to human progress in every field of endeavour (Qur'an 29:45). Practising Islam is not difficult at all. In fact, in some minor *fiqh* matters, there are differences of opinion among the *fuqaha* themselves. In extreme cases, Allah favours choices (Qur'an 5:3). This guidebook is an attempt to provide informed choices regarding topical Islamic subjects, spiritual issues and temporal matters.

I thank Allah (SWT) for guiding my hand and sustaining me with the knowledge and necessary support to undertake and complete this useful work. I pray to our Lord to provide many such opportunities to me and to others. I sincerely hope my brothers and sisters around the globe find *Islamic Perspectives on Prayers & Coping with Sickness* useful in their daily task of coping with sickness and the problems of life for themselves or when they attend to the sick and spread the message of Allah's mercy.

My sincere *Du'a-e-Maghfira* is for Abdulla Yusuf Ali and Marmaduke Muhammad Pickthall from whom I have gained much of my understanding of the Qur'an and from whose translations I have quoted in this work. *Ahadith* are mainly from the translations of Muhsin Khan and Prof. M. Mohiyuddin for *Bukhari* and from Abdul Hamid Siddiqi for *Muslim*.

"*Ya Allah*, Creator of the universe and all that is in and around it, You are *Rahmaan* and *Raheem*, You are *Shaafi* and *Baaqi*. We seek Your forgiveness and ask for refuge in You. Ward us from all calamities in this world and in the Hereafter. *Ya Allah*, guide us and keep us healthy and strong. Help us subdue *Shaitan*. Help us in our obligations and in our duties towards You as we strive to be *muttaqi* (pious) and achieve Your pleasure. *Ya Allah*, help us endure the difficulties, the suffering and the pains of disease and sickness with patience, a good countenance and a cheerful heart.

"Instill in us perseverance. You are the Curer and the Reliever. *Ya Allah*, as we advance in age and become weak and feeble, help us to cope with infirmity and make our life a pleasurable one and not a burden on others. *Ya Allah*, grant *maghfirah* for the departed ones. *Aameen*."

My wife Malika's contribution to this project is immense. She went through the drafts and revisions with me at every stage and made many wonderful suggestions. I wish to take this opportunity to thank her along with our sons Neman and Usman and our daughter Safiya for their input and help with computers.

I owe a debt of gratitude to the *Ulema* in Islamic knowledge and to several professionals who offered guidance. Among them are Nadeem Ahmed, M.D.; Haji Nazeer Ahmed; Hany K. A. Ali, Ph.D., P.Eng.; Hafiz Shaik Nafees Bhyat; Arafat El-Ashi, Ph.D.; Moulana Khaleel Sufi; Saleem Naqvi, M.D.; Shabeer A. Jeeva, M.D.; Sarah Syed, D.D.S.; and Yasmeen Shariff, M.D.

Special thanks and a debt of gratitude to Madinah University graduate Sheikh Ibrahim Malabari, whose respected authority, scholarship, personal interest and valuable insights have done much to elevate *Islamic Perspectives on Prayers & Coping with Sickness* to a respectable level. Sheikh Malabari has served on the Fiqh Council of the Islamic Society of North America.

I am ever so grateful to the Secretary General of the Canadian headquarters of the Islamic Society of North America (ISNA), Dr Mohammad Ashraf, for undertaking to publish and distribute this book. I am also grateful to Rashid Mughal for editing and designing this book in-between his own writing and teaching schedules. He has demonstrated a rare talent for words and measureless patience throughout the production of this book. May *Allah Ta'ala* bestow His choicest blessings on Brother Rashid and his family.

Finally, a word to patients: Always exercise *sabr* (patience) and never lose hope. You are never alone in your misery. Give *sadaqah* (charity). Socialize more and talk to people. Think of the Creator and praise Him through *zikr* and *tasbeeh*.

Recite the Qur'an, or listen to a recorded recitation. Since the *du'a* of a patient is very appealing to Allah (SWT), pray for yourself and for others, especially your caregivers and your medical and support staff. Be thankful to Allah (SWT). Remember that there are patients who are in worse condition than yourself! Above all, be grateful that you're of sound mind and senses and that you possess the wealth of *imaan*.

Syed Rafeeq Muhammad Amjad

A'afani min kulli daai wo aqdi a'nni haajati
Inna li qalaban saqeeman anta shaafin lil a'leel
(Arabic)

Kibr wo nakhwat jahl wo ghaflat hasad wo keena badzani
Kazab wo bad ahdi riya wo baghz wo gheebat wo dushmani
Kaun beemari hai ya Rab jo mujh men nahin!
(Urdu)

What ailment is there O! Allah that is not in me
Heal me from every illness and grant me my needs
Verily, I have a heart that is sick;
Verily, You are the Healer of the sick.
(English)

Tips for medical staff and caregivers concerning Muslim patients

The Qur'an is the revealed book of Islam.
A Muslim is a person who follows the religion of Islam.
Allah is the Creator and Lord of the Worlds.
Muhammad (PBUH) is the last prophet and messenger of Allah.

• Under a dire emergency or life-threatening situation, there are no restrictions of any kind (Qur'an 5:3) for the purposes of medication, treatment or preventative measures.

• Muslim patients should be handled, as far as possible, by medical staff of the same sex. Even the dead should be handled the same way.

• Muslims do not shake hands with the opposite sex unless they are family members or close relatives.

• Under normal conditions, mind-altering drugs and intoxicants, alcohol, pig or pork products are prohibited. At the same time, if substitutes are not available, anything is permissible including a porcine valve for the heart.

• Faith healing with *du'a* (supplication) is acceptable. Medical treatment is essential and should be undertaken for pathological and psychological disturbances.

• A Muslim recites *azan* (prayer call) in the newborn baby's right ear, and *iqama* in the left ear.

• Blood transfusion, vaccines and medications are acceptable, as are biopsies, amputations and transplants.

• Organ donations or acceptance are not restricted. However, leave this matter to the discretion of the patient's living will, or the wishes of the family.

• Genetic engineering to cure a disease is acceptable but not cloning.

• Maintaining a terminal patient on artificial life support for a prolonged period in a vegetative state is not encouraged.

• Birth control is generally acceptable on grounds of health, but the husband and wife decide what method to choose.

• Sterilization is an individual decision based on medical necessity.

• Artificial insemination is permitted if it is from husband to wife.

• Abortion is prohibited unless life is threatened.

• Circumcision is prescribed for male babies, any time after 6 days.

• A Muslim performs *wudu* (ablution), i.e., washes hands, face, wipes head and (washes) feet before each prayer of the day. If a patient cannot use water, ablution is done symbolically without water.

• If you see a Muslim patient reciting prayers in a chair or bed, leave him (or her) alone for a few minutes to finish it.

• Committed Muslim men and women follow a strict Islamic dress code even under normal conditions, requiring women to wear hijab (head scarf). Supply long gowns to ladies. Men should at least be covered all the time from the navel down to the knees.

• Muslims practise *tahara*, i.e., wash after relieving (urinating and/or passing stool). A full shower is compulsory after seminal discharge or after the end of menstrual periods or intercourse.

• Islam is based on the teachings in the Qur'an and the Traditions of Prophet Muhammad (may the peace and blessings of Allah be upon him). It is important to remember that cultural mores and news media reports do not necessarily depict true Islamic values.

• Further information regarding Islamic ethics may be obtained from the Islamic Medical Association of North America, P.O. Box 38 Plainfield, IN 46168-9904 USA (see website at http://www.imana.org) or the Islamic Society of North America, 2200 South Sheridan Way, Mississauga ON L5J 2M4, Canada via Tel (905) 403-8406 Ext. 205 or via email: isna@isnacanada.com.

Dietary Laws

• Muslim dietary laws forbid partaking of pig or pork products such as pepsin, gelatine or lard even as ingredients in food.

• Also forbidden are alcohol in food or drink and any recreational drugs, unless prescribed by a doctor for the treatment.

• Meats that are permitted include lamb, beef, chicken and turkey, slaughtered under Muslim tradition.

• Jewish kosher food is acceptable to Muslims if *halaal* meat is not available. No wine.

• All seafood (any fish), vegetables and all kinds of cereals are permitted.

Death and Burial

• When there are signs of death, inform the family about the seriousness. Friends and family members may wish to recite the Qur'an (*Surah Yaa-Seen* and *Shahada*) close to the patient at the time of death. Privacy with the family is appreciated. A Muslim *imam* or an *a'lim* (clergyman) may be called if the family so desires.

• Muslims believe in the Hereafter. When the body dies, the soul is "transferred" to the Hereafter for accountability.

• At the time of death, hospital staff are advised to adopt the following protocol:

Consult the family if available.

Turn the face in the direction of Makkah (Saudi Arabia) *if possible*.

Close the eyes of the deceased.

Close the mouth (by running gauze around the head and jaws).

Straighten arms and legs (tie toes together to keep legs straight).

Remove all tubes and needles from the body soon after death or after coroner's exam.

Release the body as soon as possible, because in keeping with Muslim tradition, the dead must be buried without unnecessary delays.

Perform an autopsy *only* if essential for any legal investigations.

• Disposal of the body follows a traditional body bath and the donning of an unstitched shroud. After a short prayer ceremony, in the mosque or elsewhere, the body is buried under Muslim custom in a Muslim cemetery without much ado or delay.

• No embalming may be done unless the body has to be flown to another country, which is discouraged.

• Cremation is prohibited in Islam.

• Organ donation is permitted, but the decision rests with the individual or collectively with the family.

Islamic Religious Concepts

• A practising Muslim follows the Qur'an and the ways of Prophet Muhammad (570-632 Christian Era). Allah is the Lord and Creator of the universe. We came from Allah and to Him shall we return.

• Every baby is a born Muslim. Subsequently, it is the influence of the parents and the environment that determines what the child will grow up to believe.

• Revelations were given to the prophets Moses, David, Jesus and Muhammad (Allah's peace be upon them all). Our source of guidance is the Qur'an, the last and final revelation given to Prophet Muhammad (PBUH). The *sunna* (or traditions) of the Prophet are the second source of guidance for Muslims, while *shariah* are the laws based on the above.

• Human beings can enter into a spiritual relationship with God. No priesthood. There is reward and punishment for the actions according to the laws in the Qur'an. Man is given power of discretion and is held responsible for his actions in this world.

• Muslims are supposed to maintain peace and harmony by greeting each other with *salaam*, to respect the beliefs of other faiths, and to respect one's parents, teachers and elders.

• Islam is best described as a way of life since religion is not separate from daily life. Men and women are equal in status and have rights and responsibilities over each other. Women get inheritance. Both have a right to divorce but it is the worst thing in the sight of Allah.

• There's no barrier of nationality, race, color, language or family status.

• Muslims stand shoulder-to-shoulder in the congregational prayer.

• In terms of personal deeds, or the foods one may eat, *halaal* (lawful) and *haraam* (prohibited) are very important to a Muslim, as they are well defined in the Qur'an and *Sunnah*.

• Family and social life are essential. Celibacy is discouraged. Recreational intoxicants, gambling, *riba* (usury), adultery, fornication, homosexuality and suicide are sinful and strictly prohibited.

Articles of Faith

• Muslims believe in Allah and in His angels, scriptures, prophets and in the Last Day. Allah is the Master of our destiny. All of us are given the power of discretion and each person is answerable for his or her deeds.

The 5 Tenets of Islam

1. Shahada: To attest and recite the creed, "There's no god but Allah; Muhammad is the messenger of Allah."

2. Salaat: To pray five times a day after a ritual ablution called *wudu*. Patients unable to stand for prayers may sit or lie down; and if they are unable to do that, they may pray with intention only.

3. Siyaam: Fasting during the month of Ramadan by abstaining from food and drink, smoking and sexual activity from before dawn to sunset. Patients, nursing mothers and the like are excused if they cannot keep the fast or if it is hard for them. They have to make up for not fasting upon regaining their health. Compensation for the infirm and terminally sick is through feeding the poor.

4. Zakaat: Obligatory charity one-fourtieth (or 2.5%) of one's extra wealth saved over a full year.

5. Hajj: Perform the pilgrimage in Makkah, if one can afford it, once in a lifetime.

Holidays

• The Islamic calendar is lunar-based and is eleven days shorter than the solar calendar.

• On Fridays, Muslims are enjoined to attend afternoon congregational prayers in a mosque.

• The month of Ramadan marks 30 days of fasting from early dawn to dusk and practising strict piety and self-control.

• The feast of *Eid-ul-Fitr* is observed on the first day of the month following Ramadan while the feast of *Eid-ul-Adha* is observed on the tenth day of the month of *Zul-Hajj*.

It is Allah, Lord and Cherisher of the worlds
Who created me, and Who guides me;
Who gives me food and drink,
and when I am sick, it is He Who cures me;
Who will cause me to die; and then to live again;
and Who, I hope, will forgive my faults
on the Day of Judgment.
(Qur'an 26:78-85)

ଔ ○ ଛ

Eat of all fruits, and follow the ways of your Lord
made easy. There comes from within their bellies a drink
(honey) of varying colors, wherein is healing for men:
Verily in this is a Sign for those who give thought.
(Qur'an 16:69)

ଔ ○ ଛ

O Allah, take away the disease.
Cure, for surely You are the One Who cures.
There's no cure but Yours.
Grant a cure that leaves no disease.
(Prophet Muhammad [PBUH], ref. Bukhari, Vol. 7 H 579)

ଔ ○ ଛ

Make use of medical treatment, for Allah has not made a
disease without appointing a remedy for it, with the
exception of one disease, namely, old age.
(Prophet Muhammad [PBUH], ref. Abu Dawud, Vol. 3 H 3846)

Auzubillahi minashaitan-ir-rajeem Bismillah-ir-Rahman-ir-Raheem

*The following questions and answers are for the benefit of patients
and individuals considered* mazoor *(disabled) in carrying out the normal
ways of* ibadaat. *For persons considered healthy and normal, only the normal
ways are prescribed. The degree of disability, known only to the patient,
is the key to any concession in* ibadaat.
— *Qur'an 75:14.*

Tahara & Wudu

(Personal Cleanliness for Prayers)

**1. There are bloodstains on my bedsheet, or, let's say, the body
exudes secretions and discharges that are *najas* (unclean) and
I cannot leave my bed, nor can the sheets be changed every so
often. How do I perform *salaat* in this bed?**

A: If you are so helpless, just ignore the situation and don't lose time,
especially when the stains have gone dry. Some Muslims make the mistake
of postponing their *salawaat*; they keep a count of their missed *salaat*
and perform *qada* when they get home.

Please note that *salaat* has to be performed there and then only. Life is
not guaranteed.

**2. Due to drawing of blood routinely from the arm vein, tiny
amounts of blood come out from the venipuncture. Does it spoil
my *wudu*?**

A: If the bleeding occurs after *wudu* is performed, you may wipe the
droplets of blood with a swab or a wet tissue to keep your *wudu* intact.
After all, wounded *Sahaba* continued *salaat* even on the battlefield!
However, if the vein starts to bleed profusely, then stanch the flow of blood
before you perform fresh *wudu*.

3. **My *wudu* keeps breaking frequently due to passing of wind and it is not practical to keep on performing *wudu*. How would I help myself to attend to *salaat*?**

A: If it's a health problem beyond your control, just perform *wudu* and start and finish *salaat* despite the situation, especially if your medical condition is uncontrollable. *Salaat* cannot be put off under any circumstances.

Two of the major causes of uncontrollable flatulence or the involuntary passing of wind are indiscriminate consumption of gas-producing foods and eating more than is necessary. If your gas problem is beyond normal, consult your physician. It can be cured.

4. **Water or water jugs are not available in many washrooms. What would you suggest to maintain *tahara* (cleanliness)?**

A: Use tissue paper. Wash yourself properly as soon as water is available. *(See Qur'an 5:6)*

5. **I have an artificial arm. Do I have to wash it as part of my *wudu*?**

A: No, wipe it clean if necessary. Wash the tip of the remaining part of the natural arm. Also, there's no need to perform *masaah* on the artificial limb.

6. **I have a leakage problem due to my bad bladder. What is the solution for *wudu* and *salaat*?**

A: There are devices available at the pharmacies for this kind of problem. An adult diaper is the answer. Whenever this is not possible or not practical and it is time for *salaat*, just perform *wudu* and *salaat* as soon as possible.

Allah (SWT) surely knows your problem and He is *Ghafoorur-Raheem* (Oft-forgiving and most Merciful).

7. **The doctor has inserted a catheter in my urinary tract and the urine-collecting bag is attached to me. How can I maintain** *tahara* **and attend to my** *salawaat* **(prayers)?**

A: This is not a normal situation. You don't have much choice and you cannot wait for hours and days without remembering the Creator, neither do you know for sure how long this is going to continue. Allah (SWT) knows your situation better. Hence, you simply perform *wudu* and carry on your obligatory prayers on time.

8. **Suppose, the** *ghusl* **has become obligatory due to** *janabah* **on me, and I cannot perform** *ghusl* **or** *wudu* **due to medical reasons. How should I perform my** *ibadaat*?

A: If you are afraid that your *salaat* will be missed because of this reason, perform *tayammum* and proceed with your *ibadaat* including *salaat*. (Qur'an 5:6)

9. **On my way to the hospital, I stopped at the mosque and performed** *salaat*. **I realized at this point that I was carrying a urine sample in a small specimen bottle in my pocket. There was no leakage of course. I want to know whether it was all right to carry the bottle in the pocket during the** *salaat*.

A: Opinions of the *ulema* differ. *Salaat* is accepted, *Insha Allah*. For the next time, remember to remove such things from your pocket before you perform *salaat*. Some scholars maintain that such a situation would render the *salaat* unacceptable.

10. **Occasionally, I notice some fluid (prostatic fluid) oozing from my penis. What do I do for the** *wudu* **and** *salaat*?

A: At this stage you are considered as *mazoor* (disabled and helpless). Wash the affected areas, and perform *wudu* before *salaat*. According to Muwatta (chapter 20, #81, page 18), *ghusl* is not necessary. I suggest you should see your doctor at once, especially if you're 50 or older.

11. **During my monthly periods, bleeding continues for a few days beyond the usual number of days. Do I take it for granted that this is part of my monthly periods and avoid my *salaat*?**

A: This problem is other than your monthly periods. At the end of your regular number of days of menstruation, take the obligatory *ghusl* and proceed with your regular *salaat*. For subsequent prayers, just perform *wudu* for *salaat*.   (See Bukhari, Vol. 1, Hadith # 228 P 146)

Continuous bleeding is an indication of some health problem. Consult your physician if bleeding persists.

12. **I am an in-patient and have to perform *wudu* in a place where staff members (male) come and go. How can I perform *masaah* on my head with my *hijab* on?**

A: In this situation, there's no need to uncover your headdress. Just perform your *masaah* over the *hijab* itself.

13. **As a hospital worker, my work involves handling all kinds of chemicals, biological fluids and specimens, which naturally include urine and fecal samples, too. Do I have to perform *ghusl* before I am ready for *salaat*?**

A: Most hospital workers, especially the laboratory personnel, wear protective outfits and follow universal precautions against infection. They are more careful, more knowledgeable and better trained than the general public. Their personal clothing — including the body — is certainly free from any contamination. A thorough *wudu* should be quite sufficient.

However, a shower at the end of the day's work is highly warranted as a precautionary measure before mingling with the family.

14. I (a lady) performed *wudu* and was all set for the *salaat*. The doctor (male) came in, checked my pulse and drew some arterial blood. Do I have to perform *wudu* once again, since this person (of opposite sex) touched me?

A: Your *wudu* is not nullified under the circumstances, since your *niyyah* (intention) is clean. Where a lady doctor or a nurse is not available, and such physical tests have to be performed for medical treatment, such touching by a doctor of the opposite sex is not a problem.

15. I was about to perform *salaat* when I vomited. Frequent vomiting has been my problem. It is rather difficult to keep performing *wudu* for a patient like me.

A: Imam Malik mentions that Malik (RA) saw Rabiah binti Abd al-Rahman vomiting out water several times. He was in the mosque and said his prayers without performing ablution. (Muwatta, p 11, ch 12, #45).

Under this guidance, one does not have to perform *wudu* after vomiting, especially after vomiting clear fluids.

On the other hand, Imam Muslim recommends that you gargle the mouth and wash the face after this kind of vomiting. In any case, do not miss *salaat*. Under normal circumstances, if you vomit actual food, then you have to perform *wudu*.

16. In my case, whenever there's nose bleeding, it is profuse. How can I manage *salaat*?

A: People with heavy nose bleeding problem should sit or lie down or say their *salaat* with a sign of the head. (Muwatta, p 17, ch 18, #80)

17. **If the nose starts bleeding during *salaat*, do I have to break the *salaat*, perform *wudu* and repeat?**

A: It is all right to continue and complete *salaat* if nosebleed is manageable. (Muwatta, ch 18, p 17)

18. **During the intravenous (I.V.) drip, especially during blood transfusion, do I consider myself not clean enough to perform *wudu* or *salaat*?**

A: In a situation like this where you have no control, performing your *salaat* should not be a problem. If you can perform full *wudu*, do it. If the I.V. tubes get in the way of pouring water on the arm(s) for *wudu*, perform *masaah* by passing wet fingers around the I.V. area to complete the *wudu*.

19. **I was given blood transfusion yesterday. I do not know whose blood it was and what food habits the blood donor had. How long do you think I should wait to resume my religious obligations like *salawaat* (daily prayers)?**

A: You do not have to wait for anything. Keep up with your routine *salaat* and other *ibadaat*. Allah (SWT) knows best about the contents of the blood running in one's body, before or after the transfusion. Your point has a value in your *taqwa*, (piety). May Allah (SWT) strengthen our *imaan* and bless us with *taqwa*. *Aameen*.

20. **The doctor wants to give blood transfusion to my mother. She does not want to take it, her reason being that this blood could be from a person with *haraam* food habits. Is there any Qur'anic injunction so I can convince my mother to accept the blood transfusion?**

A: Blood transfusion is permissible. Her medical problem seems to be a life threatening one. Given such a situation, many things become permissible. In *Surah Al-Maidah* (5:3) we read, "... whoever is forced by hunger, not by will, to sin: (for him) lo! Allah is Most Forgiving, Most Merciful." Again, in Surah 6:145 we are reminded that if you are compelled or driven by necessity, neither craving nor transgressing, being neither disobedient nor exceeding the limit, then surely the Lord is Most Forgiving and Merciful.

You should be proud to have a mother with such great *taqwa*.

Regarding blood transfusion, it is possible to give your own blood, to be stored away for your next surgery. Parents can donate their blood only to their very young children. Talk to your doctor and the Red Cross or Red Crescent authorities for details.

21. I am severely paralyzed / paraplegic / suffering from Parkinson's disease. I am temporarily / completely blind due to a recent eye operation. I cannot perform *wudu* all by myself. I cannot get help all the time either. How can I manage for my *salaat*?

A: In your condition, if you think it is time for *salaat*, just perform *salaat* the way you are. If you're so disabled, you may perform *salaat* without *wudu* with water. A blind person can perform *tayammum* on anything around him. If the patient is paraplegic, and help is not available for *wudu* or *tayammum*, offer your *salaat* as you are. Allah (SWT) knows your condition. Your good intention or *niyyah* is what is counted. Keep making *du'a* for better conditions.

Alternatively, you may keep a small slab of marble (available from a ceramic store) or a flat stone from the riverbed handy to perform *tayammum* on it.

22. How can I perform *wudu* when I cannot even get up from my bed?

A: You may ask for a wet towel from the nursing station, make your intent for *wudu* and wipe or rub yourself in lieu of running water. Remember that the least you have to do to perform *wudu* is to wash face and hands and to wipe head and [wash] feet. (Qur'an 5:6)

23. **A nurse or attendant in the hospital wants to help me perform *wudu* in my bed. But she is not a believer in Islam. The male attendant is a Muslim, but I (a lady) prefer a lady to help me. Is this *wudu* valid when done with the help of a non-Muslim?**

A: *Insha Allah*, it is all right. In fact, your choice of getting help from a person of the same sex is better.

24. **If I am not allowed to put water on my wound, and I cannot wash over the cast on my fracture, how can I perform *wudu*?**

A: You may perform *masaah* by passing wet fingers symbolically over the affected areas. For the rest of the body, regular *wudu* is required.

25. **I am told we should not wipe off the dripping water after *wudu*. I am sick and old and feel cold by practising it, especially when I am travelling during the winter season.**

A: Yes, you can wipe dry. If you lived in the desert or in places like Makkah and Madinah where daily temperatures are around 45 degrees Celsius, you'd certainly practice it! In colder countries, one does not have to follow this practice. Prophet Muhammad (PBUH) did not specifically recommend this action.

26. **Can you explain the procedure for performing *wudu* without water, what is known as *tayammum*? Do I have to have a bucket of clean sand near my hospital bed?**

A: The easiest way would be to keep a clean small flat piece of marble (or a small clean rock that can be collected at the riversides) handy in your night table. Make your intention for *tayammum*, pat your hands on the rock, and pass hands on each other. Repeat patting hands on the rock, and pass these hands on the face. (Qur'an 5:6)

A fancy marble or soapstone flower vase, stone plate or even an earthen flowerpot is quite practical.

Normally, *tayammum* is performed with a clean object that will not burn or melt, such as sand.

27. I cannot gargle or clean my nostrils with water in my hospital bed, but I can perform the rest of *wudu* with a wet towel. Is that acceptable?

A: Yes. The *fard* part of the *wudu* is described in the Qur'an (5:6) as "... wash your faces, and your hands up to the elbows, and lightly rub your hands and (wash) your feet up to the ankles." The rest of the description of *wudu* is *sunnah*, which is highly desirable but not compulsory. Hence, if running water is not within your reach, use a wet towel.

28. I wear socks after my *wudu*. It is very difficult to lift my feet in the washbasin or sink. For subsequent *wudu*, can I just perform *masaah* on the socks, instead of washing the feet again?

A: Yes, you can perform *masaah* on socks. Prophet Muhammad (PBUH) wore leather socks called *khuffs*. *Khuffs* were the custom of those days. Today, many, if not all, scholars consider cotton/polyester socks of reasonable thickness are acceptable for *masaah*. As for disabled folks, *masaah* is good enough on any part of the body on which water is not to be poured. Make sure you do not walk on a dirty wet floor in your socks. (Bukhari Vol. 1, Hadith 205; Abu Dawood Vol. 1 Chap. 62).

Masaah on the socks as described above is good for 24 hours for a resident and good for 3 days for a traveller.

Salaat (Namaz, Prayers)

29. I am in the hospital as a patient. Do I *have* to pray?

A: Surah 17, verse 82 informs us Allah has set down in the Qur'an that which is a healing and a mercy to those who believe.

Salaat (prayer or *namaz*) is compulsory for all sane adult Muslims whether in the hospital bed, on the battlefield, at work or at home. In case of extreme difficulties, one can say the *salaat* sitting down or lying down or in whatever position possible. *Salaat* distinguishes a *kafir* from a *momin*. Wilfully denying *salaat* is a great sin. (Qur'an 2:238 and Bukhari vol. 1 Hadith 527).

In *Surah Maryam*, Allah *Ta'ala* says He is "Lord of the heavens and the earth, and all that is between them: so worship Him and be constant and patient in His worship: knowest thou of any who is worthy of the same name as He?" (Qur'an 19:65)

And in *Surah Al-Mu'minun*, Allah *Ta'ala* says, "Successful indeed are the believers – those who humble themselves in their prayers." (Qur'an 23:1-2)

So, what are we waiting for when Allah *Ta'ala* is the *Shaafi*, the One Who cures? Doctors give medicines through the knowledge given by Allah *Ta'ala*. It is Allah (SWT) Who heals. So it is better for us to bow down in prostration to the One who heals and sustains us.

Besides, if one realizes what's in store in the Hereafter, especially in *Jahannam* (Hell), one would rather aspire to a longer life for extra prayers. As Prophet Muhammad (PBUH) has said, "For any trouble, worry, grief, hurt or sorrow which afflicts a Muslim – even the pricking of a thorn, Almighty Allah removes in its stead some of his sins." (Bukhari, Vol. 7 Hadith 551, p 374)

30. **I am a very sick person. Let me know the minimum requirements for my daily prayers.**

A: Two *rakat* are obligatory for *Fajr* prayer, four *rakat* for *Zuhr* prayer, four *rakat* for *Asr* prayer, three *rakat* for *Maghrib*, and four *rakat* for *Isha* prayer.

Each of these *rakats* calls for *niyyah* (intention), *qiyaam* (standing for healthy ones, sitting or in bed for the sick), recitation of *Surah Fateha*, one *ruku'u*, two *sujood* and of course, *tashahhud* and *darood.*

31. **As a patient, I have difficulty in waking up for the** *fajr* **prayer in time. Can I perform this** *salaat* **after sunrise?**

A: If it is really that difficult, it is better to perform your *fajr* late than never. Keep trying your best to be punctual and beg Allah (SWT) for forgiveness and help. You'll find great personal advantages and tremendous benediction in rising early. It should not be a habit to perform *fajr salaat* late.

32. **Can a patient perform** *salaat* **by lying down in bed, while sitting or just standing?**

A: Yes, if the patient is helpless.

33. **My baby is sick. I have to attend to her most of the time. How would I perform my own** *salaat***?**

A: Just carry the baby in your arms and perform *salaat*. You may lay the baby next to you so s/he can see you performing *salaat*.

34. **During** *salaat***, I feel giddiness while I remain standing for** *qiyaam***. Can I sit down during second** *rak'at* **if I have to, and continue my prayers? Does it require** *sujoodus-sahoo***?**

A: Yes, indeed. You can sit down any time during the *salaat* in case of a problem. Allah (SWT) is certainly aware of all the situations and He is the Most Merciful. *Sujoodus-sahoo* is not necessary. Allah (SWT) has made *ibadaat* easy for man.

35. Just like *qasr* for the travellers, is there any concession in *salaat* for the sick?

A: No, but the patient may sit or lie down and, in extreme cases, perform *salaat* by movements of fingers, head or eyes.

36. My X-ray appointments often fall during *zuhr* time around 1:30 p.m. and I have been missing this *salaat* on these days. Can I perform my *zuhr salaat* after 2.30 p.m.?

A: The time for *zuhr* begins after *zawal*, that is, after the sun begins to decline from its zenith, and lasts until it is time for *asr*. One can pray at any time during this period. It does not have to be always at 1:30 on the dot. In the same way, *asr* time extends until before *maghrib*.

Please remember that praying each *salaat* as soon as its time falls due is a practice established by Prophet Muhammad (PBUH).

37. Under hospital conditions, to keep up the appointments for the blood work, X-rays, etc., can one combine *zuhr* and *asr* together, and later, *maghrib* and *isha salaat*?

A: If it is not possible at all, then you can combine these *salaat* but don't make a habit of it.

38. When my family and friends visit me at the hospital in the evenings, time passes so quickly that they cannot keep up with their *asr* and *maghrib* prayers. Also, by then it's time for visitors to go home. What is your suggestion for place and performing

the *salaat* in time for the visitors? This is a typical situation during winter in many countries in the northern hemisphere.

A: Finding a place for *salaat* should not be a problem these days. Many hospitals and institutions in North America recognize this need and provide accommodation for such spiritual activity. There are arrangements in a worship room, lounge, quite room or chapel. Check out about the facilities available with your hospital authorities.

If such an arrangement is non-existent, you can find a quiet place outside, e.g., a park bench if the weather permits, or inside your own car while sitting.

Once you find this place, perform your *salaat* in time rather than postponing it. Chances are you might be tied up longer than you thought, or you may forget altogether. Well, if it is all extremely difficult, the only way is to reach home and perform your *salawaat*.

39. How should an infirm patient perform the *Jum'a* prayer?

A: Just perform the *zuhr salaat* at home/hospital. Trust Allah (SWT) and keep praying for better health to be able to perform your prayers in a mosque or in *jama't*.

I have come across a Muslim brother in a nursing home who is confined to his wheelchair. He promptly books his rides with special public transportation and never neglects his congregational prayers on Fridays and *taraweeh* during Ramadan. May *Allah Ta'ala* reward him.

40. I have been sick and bedridden for some time. I could not go to *masjid* for *Jum'a* prayer in the past two weeks. I am afraid I might miss it again this week.

A: You're not neglecting to go to the mosque. Keep up your *zuhr salaat*. May Allah (SWT) give you more *taqwa* and *shifa*. You do your best and leave the rest to Allah (SWT).

41. **Occasionally, my appointment with the doctor, who is a specialist, falls on Friday afternoons. I am afraid of missing alternate appointment. Is it all right for me to miss a Friday congregational prayer for this reason?**

A: Doctors know that faith in God heals people. If you explain to your physician or his/her secretary the importance of congregational prayers for you as a Muslim, they will most likely respect your wishes. If not, then offer your *zuhr* prayers afterwards instead. Missing three *Jum'a* congregational prayers in a row, without a valid reason, can have serious spiritual consequences.

42. **This year I am unlucky since I have to remain in the hospital on the day of Eid. I will be missing the prayers. Can I say my Eid prayers in my own bed that day in the hospital?**

A: Eid prayers are only *sunnah*, not mandatory, and the *Eid salaat* is not performed individually at home or in the hospital. Indeed, you will be missing a big congregational prayer and meeting your friends there.

43. **Can I keep my eyes closed during *salaat* either for concentration, to avoid being distracted by hospital visitors, or simply because of my physical weakness?**

A: Normally, it is not advisable to close your eyes during *salaat*. In any case, your *salaat* will remain valid if you keep your eyes closed, especially if it aids you to concentrate better in your *ibadah*.

43. **I wear thick eyeglasses. When I go into *sujood*, I can only rest my forehead or the nose on the floor, and not both at the**

same time. My friend says that my *salaat* is not right and I am advised to remove my glasses during my *salaat*. I do not feel comfortable about this since it's difficult for me to go without my spectacles. What is your suggestion?

A: Your friend's observation is valid. Under normal situations, during *sujood* one has to rest on toes, both knees, both palms, nose and forehead. Given your condition, do your best. Wear your glasses and place forehead only on the ground.

44. **I have a wound on my forehead. I cannot rest my forehead on the floor during the *sajda*. Does Allah (SWT) accept this *salaat*?**

A: *Insha Allah*, yes. Rest your nose on the floor and not your forehead. Allah (SWT) knows your difficulty and intention.

45. **I have great difficulty in standing for *salaat*, so I sit down. But do I get more virtues if I still stand in pain and perform *salaat*?**

A: We do not have to exert ourselves beyond our capacity. Allah has made the *deen* easy to practise.

46. **Since I am feeling weak, can I perform my *fard salaat* in the prescribed way and the *sunna salaat* by sitting down?**

A: Yes, as a matter of fact, you may perform all your prayers in the sitting or lying positions till you are strong enough.

47. **What if a patient prepares for *salaat*, but cannot complete it each time due to weakness?**

A: Do your best and leave the rest to Allah. Intention is the main thing.

48. **My father is old and weak yet he keeps up with his regular** *salawaat*. **Do you think he's getting enough exercise through his praying?**

A: Every little movement helps elderly people. Dr Shahid Athar reports, "Movements in the *salaat* are mild, uniform and involve all muscles and joints." (Ref. *Islamic Horizons*, April 1986). Some older folks are obliged to make physical movements in the name of *salaat*. Otherwise, they might sit idle!

49. **In a hospital setting, what is the best place or area to perform** *salaat* **by patients who are able to walk around?**

A: You can go to the prayer room (quiet room, meditation room, chapel, or a meeting room) in that hospital. But make sure the nurse knows your whereabouts. Better still, pray by your bedside. This is important because a patient could fall unconscious anywhere any time for any reason, or you might be in need of personal emergency assistance, or the nurse might be looking for you for some treatment, so why not pray by your bedside!

50. **A patient often forgets the number of** *rakaat* **during his** *salaat*.

A: In case of doubt, perform *sujoodus-sahoo* at the end.

51. **I am weak and have a problem sitting on the hard floor. Can I sit on a chair and yet join the congregational** *salaat* **in the mosque?**

A: Sure, pick up a chair and lay it on the extreme right side of the line. If you're sitting on the floor, take the extreme right spot; since the line starts from the right, you will be saved from the hassle of shifting your place.

52. I was all set for *salaat*, and then supper was served on the hospital bed. (a) Do I have to say *salaat* first before I eat, or can I eat first since I am hungry?   (b) Do I have to perform *wudu* once again, because I ate?

A: (a) Eat first. (Ref. Muwatta by Imam Malik, ch 13, #47, page 11). (b) No. The Prophet of Allah (PBUH) would rinse his mouth after eating and before performing *salaat*. (Ref. Bukhari Vol. 1, Hadith # 208, P 138.)

It is interesting to note here that after eating camel's meat, one is supposed to perform *wudu*.

53. I have to rub medicine on my scalp, so I cannot wear a headdress (cap) for the *salaat*. What should I do?

A: Headddress for men is not necessary. Ladies, however, have no option but to wear *hijab*. If it comes in the way of medical treatment, with no other option, go without headdress. Allah (SWT) knows your situation.

54. I am suffering from a cold, and my nose is running profusely. I have to keep wiping it dry during my *salaat*. Can I wipe my nose every now and then during the *salaat*? Let me know whether I have to perform *sujoodus-sahu* for my actions?

A: It is better to keep wiping the nose during *salaat*. *Sujoodus-sahoo* is not warranted. During the *salaat*, the actions, other than the prescribed movements should remain minimal. An onlooker should not mistake the actions of a *musalli* (one who is praying) as part of the *salaat*.

55. Hospital patients are given examination gowns to wear and I do not feel comfortable in them especially when it comes to praying. It does not cover *satr* (minimum clothing to cover, as prescribed in Islam). What do I do?

A: The most minimum cover (*satr*) for men is between the navel and the knees, even for *salaat*. For women, the maximum exposure for *salaat* or outside the home is face, hands and feet. This is relaxed in the company of ladies only or with the *mahram*. For *salaat*, ladies have to have complete *satr*.

If it is not in the way of your treatment or examination time, I am sure the medical staff would not mind you wearing the pajamas and *hijab* to cover the *satr*. A housecoat or a robe would be appropriate if you have to move about.

Narrated Muhammad bin Al-Munkadir: I went to Jabir bin Abdullah, and he was praying wrapped in a garment and his *rida* (a large covering sheet) was lying beside him. When he finished the prayers, I said, "O Abdullah! You pray (in a single garment) while your *rida* is lying besides you?" He replied, "Yes, I did it intentionally so that the ignorant ones like you might see me. I saw the Prophet (PBUH) praying like this." (Bukhari, Vol. 1, Hadith # 366)

56. I feel shy to perform *salaat* in the hospital or outside home (except in the *masjid*). So, can I postpone all my *salawaat* until after I return home from the hospital?

A: Shyness for *salaat* in public places is one of the signs of weakness in *imaan* and the commitment to submit to the Will of our Creator. It does take a bit of courage the first few times. Then you acquire an immunity to the ignorant comments of people. Chances are that your *salaat* may give some food for thought to the onlookers. This is a *da'wah* (invitation to Islam).

Salaat has to be performed at the prescribed time. The whole earth is made a permissible place for *salaat*. Remain in contact with the Creator and be aware of your duties.

57. **If I am in the middle of my *salaat* in the hospital bed or chair and if a visitor, nurse or doctor comes in and tries to talk to me, can I break my *salaat* and ask this person to come back later? Can I ask them to wait using sign language?**

A: It is better to leave a sign near the door or the bed in advance saying "Praying" or "Meditating" or "Do not disturb." If you have not left a message earlier, sign language is the answer. If there is any confusion with the sign, communicate with the person and then repeat the *salaat* later. Allah (SWT) is *Ghafoorur-Raheem*. (Ref. Muslim Vol.1, P 273 H # 1101)

58. **I know that ladies are exempted from *salaat* during childbirth and later confinement. But do they have to perform *qada* to make good for the missing *salawaat* at a later date?**

A: No. It is the blessing and the grace of Allah (SWT).

59. **Is it all right to ask my family to perform *fard salaat* on my behalf when I am very sick?**

A: *Salaat* is a personal responsibility of every sane adult Muslim. That is one of the reasons perhaps *salaat* is made easy to perform by all the people, at all times, in any place.

60. **Can I perform *fard salaat* on my (late) parents' behalf, which they might have missed during their lifetime, in order to repay for their kindness? Also tell me if I can do anything else for them now?**

A: No one can perform *salaat* on someone else's behalf. Just make *Du'a-e-Magfirah* for the dead. As Prophet Muhammad (PBUH) has taught us, one way to pay back to our parents is by being righteous, giving charity on their behalf, and even by performing *hajj* on their behalf. Remember and recite the *du'a*, "My Lord! Bestow on them (parents) Your Mercy as they did bring me up when I was small." (Qur'an 17:24)

61. Why is *salaat* so important even for the sick patients in the hospitals?

A: *Salaat* is the second pillar of Islam and its performance differentiates between a believer and a non-believer.

According to the Qur'an, *salaat* keeps one away from indecencies, and keeps one closer to the Creator. One of the best quotations that I can think of from the Qur'an points out that *salaat* prevents us from every kind of sin, disbelief and evil. Also, it says that remembering Allah is the greatest indeed. Allah is always watching us. (Qur'an 29:45)

The patient gets *sukoon* (tranquility) during and after *salaat*. Sickness is the test for otherwise healthy, weakness is the test for otherwise strong, poverty is the test for otherwise a rich man, by the Almighty. Use Allah's bounties (health, strength, wealth, etc.), wisely. We are all responsible for our deeds and answerable for the bounties of Allah. (Qur'an 102:8)

It is interesting to note here as reported by Dr Basim A M Alnafoosi, Dept. of Rheumatology, Saddam General Hospital, Mosul Iraq, (Supplement to JIMA Vol. 24 July 1992) that "Early age Islamic praying and continuation decreases symptoms of backache."

As translated by Yusuf Ali, it says in the Qur'an (13:28, 17:82), "... in the remembrance of Allah do hearts find satisfaction, tranquility, healing and mercy."

62. A Muslim volunteer came to me in hospital and talked to me about prayers five times a day and daily. I am already a sick man and do I have to go through this now? Can you enlighten me about this, please?

A: One should be thankful to Allah for sending someone to remind us of our duties and obligations to ourselves and to others. Human beings have a body and a soul; these represent the physical and the spiritual aspects of our being. Both have to survive, grow, flourish, remain healthy, successful and be worthy of being created. They need nourishment, exercise and guidance to achieve excellence and to be answerable for our actions in this world. Our physical needs are food, clothing and shelter; but for our spiritual growth we need to study, understand, and practise our faith to our utmost capacity.

It is therefore important to know and understand the real meaning of prayer. Merely standing, bowing, sitting or prostrating oneself does not achieve any real purpose. Realizing your Creator and bowing to Him in submission in prayers is the way to success here and in the Hereafter. Sincere *salaat* is not only food for the soul but it shields the body from temptations and other evils in our worldly lives.

Our *salaat* creates a rapport between Allah and ourselves, and the Messenger of Allah has taught us to renew our covenant with Allah. Thus it is essential for us to stay in constant and frequent touch with Allah. In fact *salaat* marks the difference between a believer and a non-believer. *Salaat* shields us from Satan's wicked ways. The more our understanding of Allah grows, the more inner joy, tranquility and success we are likely to derive from our devotions and supplications. Surely, Allah does not need our *salawaat*; it is we who need His mercy to protect us from *Shaitan* and to guide us to success.

Finally, as Prophet Muhammad (PBUH) himself has noted, "If there was a river at the door of anyone of you and he took a bath in it five times a day, would you notice any dirt on him? This is the example of the five prayers with which Allah (SWT) annuls evil deeds." (Bukhari, Vol. 1, Hadith # 506, P 301)

63. **There is a patient who is unconscious for most of the time. He regains consciousness occasionally. What is the injunction for his *salaat*?**

A: If the consciousness comes at regular time of the day (e.g. every morning), then the past prayers of the day are due. If the consciousness comes occasionally, the *salaat* is performed for that time only. The rest of the *salawaat* during unconsciousness are not necessarily due.

64. **I was unconscious for one whole day. Should I make up the missed *salawaat*?**

A: If a patient remains unconscious for a period of time that covers five consecutive prayers, none of the *salaat* is due later. The patient is deemed mentally incapacitated, and therefore exempt from prayer. But, if the unconsciousness is of a shorter duration than five consecutive *salawaat*, then the missed prayers become due. For that matter, having regained consciousness after such a long period, I would offer as many *nafl* prayers as possible to thank Allah for His gift of health.

65. **During my major surgery, I was incapable of performing *salaat* at all. In fact I did not even think of *salaat*. What are the prescribed injunctions concerning *ibadaat* under such circumstances?**

A: *Salaat* is compulsory -- even on one's deathbed. May Allah guide and give us strength and courage to carry out our *faraiz*. Under such helpless conditions, the least one can do to perform *salaat* is to make *niyyah*, and use whatever part of the body is moveable to represent the actions of the *salaat*. One can do this by moving the fingers or the head. The angels may even plead with the Lord to accept such an effort as an acceptable *salaat*.

Abdullah bin Umar reported that the Prophet (PBUH) said: "Whenever a person gets sick (who has difficulty in performing *ibadaat* physically), his deeds are recorded for him in accordance with what he used to do when he was well." (Ref: Bukhari, in al-Adabul-Mufrad # 501)

66. Do hospitals have places reserved for prayers?

A: Most hospitals have a designated room for prayer, personal solace or meditation, variously called chapel, quiet room, prayer room or multifaith worship room. You may also contact any Muslim employees there to ask what they do for their daily prayers; or you can ask nursing staff for a place to pray. They do their best to oblige.

Hospital chapels are good enough for our *salaat*. In fact, some good Muslims donate prayer mats to the chapels in hospitals. If you don't find a prayer mat or a copy of the Qur'an in your hospital chapel, donate one.

Ibn Abbas would pray in a church provided there were no statues in it. (Ref. Bukhari, Vol. 1, chapter 54, P 254)

Ramadan & Fasting

67. During the month of Ramadan, what is the ruling concerning fasting for a sick person like myself?

A: If the doctor restricts fasting for the purpose of treatment, or he ascertains that fasting is detrimental to the health of the patient, then it can certainly be postponed till health is regained. A Muslim doctor may even recommend that one abstain from fasting for the rest of one's life for health reasons. In such a case, *fidya* will have to be given, that is, feeding one person (or paying for the meal) for every missed *sawm* (fast). (Qur'an 2:184)

68. I suffer from stomach ulcers and cannot fast during the month of Ramadan.

A: You have raised a good question because it is obvious that fasting in Ramadan is a provocative test for a latent disease, as mentioned by Dr Bakir (JIMA, vol. 22 # 4 P 184, Oct. 1990).

It would be prudent to consult a doctor knowledgeable in Islam regarding the severity of your medical problem. If the doctor says no, you are exempted from fasting. Respect the month of Ramadan by practicing all the requirements of the *siyaam* except being hungry. However, *fidya* is due.

69. **Usually I pay my *zakaat-ul-maal* and *zakat-ul-fitr* during the month of Ramadan. This year, during Ramadan, I am hospitalized. Can I go back home after the recovery, and then distribute my *zakat* and *fitra* later, maybe next month?**

A: You have to pay *fitra* before *Eid*. Regarding *zakaa*, if you are unable to calculate, take assistance, make the family aware of it and disburse later. It is better to calculate and disburse the dues beforehand. Do not postpone a *fard* (mandatory task), as there's no guarantee of life! It is only *fitra* that has to be paid during Ramadan, before the *Eid-ul-Fitr* congregational prayer. *Zakaat*, which is due annually, may be calculated and disbursed on any day of the year. Generally, Muslims select the month of Ramadan because this is the month of more blessings.

Here are two interesting websites: www.soundvision.com/life/zakatcalc.shtml; and www.al-huda.ca/index.html

70. **I am a hospital worker. It so happened that our department arranged for us to be vaccinated against hepatitis during the month of Ramadan. Can I take this vaccine while I am fasting?**

A: If it isn't possible to get it done after Ramadan, get it now. Injections that have no food value, except for a few drops of water. This does not affect your fast. Let's not split hairs! After all, it is one's intention that is paramount here, like one's attitude.

71. Can I take injections containing vitamins or calcium, vaccines and the like when I'm fasting since I cannot postpone these injections to a later time?

A: There should be no problem, *insha Allah*, with injections of no food value giving you energy or keeping you from feeling hungry or thirsty — especially when these are not taken by mouth.

72. To keep up the health of my body and soul, I want to offer extra *nafl siyaam*. Which are the best days?

A: Fasting in the month of Ramadan is compulsory to develop *taqwa* (piety). It is healthy only if the stomach is not overloaded. Other than Ramadan, Prophet Muhammad (PBUH) is reported to have fasted on Mondays, Thursdays and Full Moon days, which are the 13th, 14th and 15th of the lunar calendar, the 9th and 10th or 10th and 11th of *Muharram*, any six days during the month of *Shawwaal*, and the day of *Arafaat* (for those not performing *hajj* at that time).

73. I have to take a new prescription for eyeglasses. The optometrist wants to drop some medicine in my eyes. Can I get it done while I am fasting?

A: These eye drops contain a dye and a medicine to dilate pupils for examination. It is all right to get it done and it will not affect your fast in any way.

74. Can I take allergy shots during fasting time?

A: By taking allergy shots while fasting, your system gets a few drops of moisture. This has no nutritional value. This should be all right only if you cannot go without it or get it postponed. However, flu shot contains traces of pig's gelatin. Since there is no choice without this, and this being essential for health, it is all right to take the shot. (Qur'an 5:3)

75. **During Ramadan I experience occasional bad breath. How can I overcome this problem?**

A: The problem of bad breath is mostly due to neglected dental care. It will be a good idea to go to the dentist before Ramadan, discuss the problem and get this treated.

After *sahoor*, brush your teeth and run floss *(khilal)*. Prophet Muhammad (PBUH) did *khilal*, rinsed his mouth and brushed his teeth with *miswak*, a brush made from the root of a plant known as *Salvadora persica*. The use of *miswak* keeps gums clean and healthy. If the problem persists, see the dentist immediately after Ramadan.

Let's not forget that the mouth contains innumerable bacteria even under normal conditions. Anaerobic bacteria lodge and grow on the tongue and between teeth and gums. They produce bad odour and cause gum diseases. During Ramadan, you may brush your teeth with baking powder or powdered charcoal during daytime but make sure you do not swallow anything during your fast. Charcoal absorbs odours and has no food value.

If you have to use your regular toothpaste, which usually has very small quantity of artificial sugar, use it sparingly and quickly rinse mouth to avoid taste.

The tongue cleaner is a very interesting little tool to get rid of bad breath. With this thin plastic or blunt steel blade, half a centimetre wide and about 15cm long, you scrape the tongue from the back of the mouth to the tip of the tongue. The idea is to scrape the tongue clean of bacterial colonies that thrive there and produce bad odour. Rinse the mouth with warm water frequently (at 2-hour intervals) when fasting and you'll be amazed at the difference it makes. Make sure that you do not swallow water during this cleansing.

Mouthwashes may contain alcohol. You cannot depend on it entirely.

Keep the mouth clean, and you will not displease your family or friends.

Following are some relevant *ahadith*:

"The odour from the mouth of a person who is fasting is better to Allah than musk." (Bukhari Vol.3 P65 H # 118 & 128: Bukhari Vol. 7 P530 H # 811; Bukhari Vol. 9, P 434 H # 584; Muslim Vol. 2 P 558 H # 2564)

"One should clean his teeth before going for Jum'a prayers." (Bukhari Vol.2 P3 H # 5)

"If I did not think (that it is going to be) hard, I would have ordered cleaning of teeth (brushing) for every prayer." (Bukhari Vol. 2 P6 H # 12, Bukhari Vol. 9 P261 H # 346, Muslim Vol.1 P 158 H # 487, Abu Dawud Vol. 1 P 11 Hadith # 46)

"The prayer, where teeth have been cleaned with *miswak* is superior to other prayers by 70 times." (Ref. Baihaqi)

Hajj

76. **I saved money to go for** *hajj*, **but now I am sick. I do not know what to do.**

A: May Allah (SWT) reward you generously for your efforts. When you recover, *Insha Allah*, save money for *hajj* next year. If your illness persists and you think you'd be too weak to perform *hajj*, you may assign a family member or someone else to perform *hajj* on your behalf. This is *hajj* by proxy.

The nominee should have already performed his or her own *hajj*. It is worth noting that the *hajj* itself can be strenuous at times, so one's health and personal determination are essential factors.

77. I need cosmetic surgery, which is not a life-threatening problem. It costs quite a bit of money. I also have to perform *hajj*. I cannot afford to do both at the same time. Now I am puzzled as to which of the two should I do first?

A: You may have guessed my answer: Perform *hajj* first. Since your cosmetic surgery is not a matter of life and death, it can be postponed. *Hajj* is mandatory for every Muslim who has sufficient means to undertake the journey and who is in good health. Besides, please remember there's no guarantee of life!

78. I am chronically ill. I have saved money for *hajj*. Unfortunately I am not able to perform *hajj* in my lifetime. What should I do?

A: Arrange with a *haajj* (preferably a family member or relative) to perform the pilgrimage on your behalf as soon as possible. If immediate arrangements cannot be made, it is advisable to write so in your will.

79. I'm suffering from tuberculosis, and it is now getting contagious. I have never performed *hajj* and wonder if I can I go on *hajj* since I am strong enough to walk around?

A: A patient with a contagious disease should never mingle with others. Out of consideration for others, it would be unwise of you to go on *hajj*. In your case, *hajj* by proxy is recommended.

Consider the Hadith, "If you hear of an outbreak of plague in a land, do not enter it; but if the plague breaks out in a place while you are in it, do not leave that place." (Bukhari, Vol.7, H 624.)

80. If I fall sick (or have my monthly periods) during the *hajj* season, how should I carry on to perform *hajj*?

A: If you're sick and have not finished your *umra* or *tawaful qudoom*, and if it's time to proceed to Arafaat for *hajj*, just proceed to Arafaat. After coming back for *tawaf-e-ziarat*, women have to wait until cleared of their periods. If *tawaf-e-wida* is not possible, for whatever reason, it is all right as it's not an essential part of the *hajj*.

For details of *hajj* and *umra* for sick persons and women, please refer to books regarding *hajj* and *umra*.

Qibla

81. In the hospital room, how can I find *qibla*, the direction of prayer corresponding to the Ka'aba in Makkah, in order to say my prayers?

A: Observe the path of the sun or ask the hospital staff about the direction of North, then decide. It also helps to buy a wristwatch strap that comes with a compass attached.

82. In the hospital room, how should I manage my *salaat* if there's a picture of a person or an animal hanging on the wall facing the *qibla*?

A: Place some article, a chair or a piece of cloth, in front of you in that direction and conduct your prayer. If you're helpless to do that, just proceed with your *salaat* by focusing your sight on the spot where you would prostrate for your *sujood*.

83. I cannot face *qibla* for my *salaat* while in bed, chair or even standing because the position of the other patient in my room is in that direction. I cannot move out from my room either. Can I face another direction and proceed anyway?

A: Keep some portable object like chair or even a towel in front of you and stand for *salaat*. In a case where you are totally helpless, just perform your *salaat* in the best possible way you can with the *qibla* in mind and your intention steadfast. This is better than missing the *fard*. (Qur'an 2:177.)

84. In the hospital, my bed is set in such a way that I have to stretch my feet towards *qibla*. What do I do?

A: It is not with disrespect that you're doing so; you are helpless under the management of others. If direction cannot be easily changed, you cannot do anything about it. After all, it is not intentional. (Qur'an 2:177.)

Qur'an

85. Can you suggest some verses for hope and patience from the Qur'an, which I can recite during my illness?

A: May Allah (SWT) the *Shaafi* help you. Prophet Muhammad (PBUH) is reported to have said in a *hadith Qudsi*: "When Allah created the creatures, He wrote in the Book which is with Him in the highest heaven: 'My mercy shall prevail over My anger.'" (Ref. Muslim & Bukhari)

Refer and practice as much as you can the last verse of *Surah Al-Imran* (3:200), that says, "O ye who believe! Endure, outdo all others in endurance, be ready and observe your duty to Allah, in order that ye may succeed." (See also Qur'an 2:214; 9:129; 10:62-65; 13:11; 21:83; and 39:53-61)

It is very interesting to read some passages of *Surah Al-Shu'ara* (26:78-87) with its *tafsir*, especially 26:82 which reads, "I hope Allah will forgive me my faults on the Day of Judgment."

Please refer to the notes on the virtues of *sabr* (patience) at the end of this book.

86. Are there any medicines mentioned in the Qur'an and the books of Hadith?

A: Yes. The Qur'an itself and honey are mentioned (16:69, 17:82) as "a healing and a mercy." Reference books are available on this subject, e.g., *Natural Healing with the Medicine of the Prophet,* by Muhammad Al-Akili, ISBN 1-879405-07-5.

Also please refer to *Islamic Perspectives in Medicine – A Survey of Islamic Medicine: Achievements & Contemporary Issues* by Shahid Athar, MD, and other websites.

Books of Hadith, too, contain certain information as in Bukhari Vol. 7, chapter 71 under the title "Book of Medicine".

87. Hospital wards are not clean places to store the Qur'an and prayer mat. What would you suggest for *ibadaat*?

A: You are right to bring up this point. To Muslims, the Qur'an is "the Speech of Allah" and we revere this book and hold it dearly in all respects because it is unlike any other book. In the hospital situation, a copy of the Qur'an could be stored in or on the night table, or in some other easily accessible place like a windowsill.

A prayer mat is not a requirement for *salaat* and if you like to have it with you in the hospital, sure, store it in your locker or near your pillow. In fact, come to think of it, you can just pick up a clean towel from the hospital and perform your *salaat* on it.

88. Can I touch the Qur'an when I am without *wudu* or when *ghusl* was required while in hospital?

A: A Muslim is supposed to touch the Qur'an with *wudu*. However, if the circumstances are such that you either touch with all due respect, read and get the knowledge out of it, or lose the opportunity, I would rather hold the Qur'an in my hands and use it with respect without *wudu* but certainly not when *ghusl* is required.

Please refer to the Qur'an (56:77-79), and Maulana Maudoodi's commentary on it.

89. Can I recite Qur'an by heart without *wudu* or *ghusl*? How about *tasbeeh*?

A: Yes, you can recite the Qur'an by heart without *wudu*. However, if one is unclean, until the *ghusl* is performed, *tasbeeh* or other *zikr* (remembering or praising Allah (SWT)) may be done. (Qur'an 56:77-79).

Islam is very practical and flexible. There are no strict regulations for a patient who is helpless, and it is rather interesting what Maulana Moududi has to say about this in the Qur'an, as noted above.

90. The patient in the adjacent bed is a non-Muslim who wants to read the Qur'an. The copy of the Qur'an that I have with me contains Arabic and English text. Can I let him touch it?

A: The best thing would be to present a copy of the English translation only. The Qur'an explicitly tells us to touch it in a state of *tahara* (cleanliness), as in Qur'an 56:79. Here again, Maulana Maudoodi's *tafsir* (commentary) is quite lenient in this matter (with or without *wudu*).

Tahara injunctions in the Qur'an are for Muslims. *Tahara* and *wudu* regulations do not apply to non-believers. It is the duty of every Muslim to disseminate the message of Islam.

Food

91. My doctor has prescribed some capsules for me. I wonder if the capsule shells contain gelatin or some other animal product that is *Haraam* to eat. What should I do?

A: Find out from your pharmacist about the substance used to make these capsules. The pharmacist will be pleased to serve you, but it may not be so easy for him to be able to come up with an answer. If the capsules are made out of gelatin, ask the pharmacist whether you can get these capsules made out of starch or other acceptable product, or in a tablet form. Inquire about substitute medicines also. If none of them are available, there's nothing you can do but to take them. Allah is the best of all forgivers. (Qur'an 5:3, 6:145)

92. Doctors want me to eat Jell-O for my diet. But I know that this is made from gelatin, a pork product. How can I avoid this food?

A: Jell-O is available in a vegetarian version of gelatin, kosher Jell-O is not necessarily made from vegetables. However, Jell-O is not a medicine. A substitute can be taken. Jell-O is light, easily digestible, gives some energy, and it tastes good too!

93. I am given "vegetable" soup but who knows what it actually contains (in fact, any meat might have been used to make the broth)!

A: Inform the nurse or the dietician about your dietary requirements. The hospital will respect your needs. You can always ask the dietitian about the ingredients of any food given to you.

Note: Pea soup and Caesar salad may contain bits of pork but, these days, many hospitals refrain from pork products in their food supplies.

94. How do I know that the bread and other foods supplied in the hospitals do not contain lard?

A: Ask the nursing staff to get the information for you. Best thing is to inform the staff at the time of admission or as soon as possible about your diet regulations. No pork products, like lard, gelatin or pepsin, and no alcohol or mind-altering intoxicants except as a medical necessity.

95. Hospital meals are not cooked with *halaal* meat. What should we do?

A: Some learned Muslims suggest that under very difficult circumstances, meats (beef, lamb, chicken, etc.) supplied by the supermarkets these days in North America are acceptable; and there are those who say that is not acceptable. This is a matter of conscience. If *halaal* food is not available, then ask for *kosher* food. Watch out for wine!

Any seafood is *halaal*. Duly prepared kosher meat is acceptable. No matter what, never forget to mention the name of the *Raziq* (the Feeder, the Provider); say *Bismillah* before you eat or drink anything.

96. All my life, I was brought up with spicy food. In the hospital, I have a hard time eating the bland food.

A: With the consent of your physician, you can certainly get your meals from home.

97. I am an in-patient, away from my family. I like to eat something different from the hospital meals.

A: If the doctor has no objection for the food other than the required diet, you can always call a restaurant for your favorite food. Look up in the phone book.

98. I am told to drink milk. Are there any *aadaab* (etiquette) of drinking milk?

A: Prophet Muhammad (PBUH) would sit down to drink anything, and in small portions (except the water of *zam-zam*). He rinsed his mouth after drinking milk. Ibn Abbas (RA) narrates that "Allah's Messenger (PBUH) drank milk, rinsed his mouth and said, it has fat." (Ref. Bukhari Vol. 7, H # 514 page 354)

99. Has Allah mentioned any particular foods in the Qur'an?

A: All fruits in general. Furthermore, "...And from the fruits of date palm and grapes you get wholesome drink and nutrition: behold, in this is also a sign for those who are wise." Honey is especially confirmed to carry "healing effects". Milk is mentioned as a good food. The fruits of *Jannah*, as mentioned in *Surah Ar-Rahmaan*, are dates, grapes and pomegranates. (Qur'an 43:73 and 16:67, 69)

Fruits are low in calories (compared to cane-sugar), high in vitamins, minerals and fiber. As reported by Dr Anderson (cited by Dr Shahid Athar), fructose has been found to cause no significant rise in blood sugar: rather it was found to lower the high blood pressure of diabetics. (Ref: *Islamic Horizons*, April 1986)

100. Medicines might contain alcohol, intoxicants or even pork products as intrinsic factor. How do I avoid taking them? What about porcine heart valve?

A: Inform the physician or the nurses about your religious beliefs and dietary laws at the time of your admission. Say no to intoxicants, alcohol or pork products in any quantity or form. If it's impossible for the doctor to oblige, and if there are no substitute medications for your treatment, then you shouldn't worry at all. Allah (SWT) knows what's best for you, so accept the available medicines.

Make sure to inform the doctor that the religion of Islam prohibits alcohol and mind-altering drugs under "normal" conditions. The Merciful Creator allows using the *Haraam* under extreme situations, including the porcine heart valve. (Qur'an 6:145[146])

101. I am suffering from pernicious anemia. In order to rectify the problem of malabsorption of vitamin B$_{12}$ the doctor has prescribed an intrinsic factor made from a pig's stomach. The doctor and I have no alternatives.

A: Under the conditions described above, you are helpless. To keep up a healthy life, one is permitted to cross the limits of *haraam* and take this medicine especially when there's no substitute. (Qur'an 6:[145] 146)

Health & General Hygiene

102. **As a man, I don't think it is hygienic to sit on the toilet seat in public washrooms to urinate and wash up. The toilet seats are often dirty and there's always a possibility of back-splash from the toilet bowl. What can one do to maintain *tahara*?**

A: If you are bothered by such a situation, use the standing-style urinal. If you need to sit, lay a couple of toilet tissues on the seat, and flush the toilet bowl before using it. Keep using dry and wet towels alternately to clean yourself as best you can.

On one occasion, the Prophet himself reportedly discharged urine near a dump while standing and then performed *wudu*. (Bukhari vol. 1, Hadith # 224, P 144)

103. **How could I have remained healthy and not ended up in the hospital?**

A: Most health problems are due to an imbalance of wholesome foods coupled with bad eating habits, inadequate exercise and a poor environment. Prophet Muhammad (PBUH) recommended that we eat one-third, drink one-third and keep our stomach one-third empty!

Thank Allah for your good health. Follow the correct way of life that Islam teaches, and practice it truthfully. Eat a lawful and balanced diet (Qur'an 2:168); commit no excesses (Qur'an 20:81); and enjoy good nourishment (Qur'an 16:67). Prophet Muhammad (PBUH) has mentioned that a healthy man carries a crown on his head. Only the sick can see it!

Annual medical check-ups should be done regularly. It is essential for women to have mammograms tests around age 40. Women over 50 should have mammograms annually. Men after 50 should get tested for prostrate cancer. These problems are fairly common and early detection provides better prospects of an effective cure.

If you are sick due to flu or any contagious problem, do not go to the masjid or a friend's place. If you meet someone in this condition, take extra care. Perfect *wudu* habits can keep you from many problems. One should stop worrying and start living.

104. I think I'm getting old and weak and would rather take precautions regarding my health. Can you guide me, please?

A: Thinking you're growing old and weak is indeed wrong. Think positively, develop a good attitude, and trust in Allah (Qur'an 30:54). Get any health problem diagnosed early and get it treated. The first indication of a health problem could manifest while practicing your routine *ibadaat*. For example, if you start getting hurt in any of the hundreds of joints during the *salaat*, investigate. If you notice any giddiness or unusual palpitation of the heart during *sujood* or *qiyaam*, or back pain during *rukuu*, or if you find it difficult to fast, you should speak to your family doctor. While brushing your teeth, if your gums bleed or you suffer from excessive bad breath, see a dentist. It could be just a temporary problem, or the beginning of a serious one. If possible, see also *Journal of Islamic Medical Association* (Vol 22 #4, p 184 Oct 1990) for some very interesting comments.

105. Has any study been conducted specifically concerning health and religion?

A: Following is the research report given by *The Christian Science Monitor* not too long ago about the impact of religion (on patients):

☑ Greater religious involvement has been associated with lower blood pressure, fewer strokes and lower rates of death from heart surgery and longer survival in general.

☑ A strong religious faith and active involvement in a religious community appear to be the combination most consistently associated with better health.

☑ People with more religious experience, greater well being and life satisfaction, less depression and less anxiety, are much less likely to commit suicide.

☑ Therapies for depression and anxiety that incorporate religious beliefs in treatment result in faster recovery from illness than do traditional therapies.

☑ Heart surgery patients, who were religious, had 20% shorter post-operative hospital stays than non-religious patients in a 1987 study.

☑ Heart surgery patients assigned chaplain intervention averaged two days shorter length of stay in hospital in a 1995 study.

Such research findings have appeared elsewhere too. Gardening is also extremely beneficial for general and mental health.

106. **I am healthy but physically disabled due to my accident a few years ago. For the rest of my life, I have got to depend on someone for quite a few of my needs. I am physically challenged; at the same time, I feel very much for people who help me.**

A: Thank the Lord that you're healthy, that you can think, speak and give thanks. Make *du'a* for someone who helps you and practise *sabr*. You will be rewarded abundantly for your patience.

All of us have duties, rights and responsibilities to one another. Almost invariably, there are some people who need help and some can afford to help. Those who serve the needy, get their reward from Allah. You're giving an opportunity to someone who serves to get nearer to Allah. Here's a lesson for the healthier and physically able person to say *Shukr Alhamdulillah* for his/her own health and fitness. A smart person would rather become humble and get rid of his/her ego or pride just by looking at you. We are human beings; we have to learn to live in peace and harmony by helping each other.

This is also a matter of *qadr* (fate). Only Allah knows why He does something like this to someone. You do not have to feel inferior or helpless in any way. Certainly, it is your obligation to make a very sincere *du'a* for anyone who helps you.

107. **Can you suggest simple hygiene for the visitors of patients?**

A: *Rasool Allah* (PBUH) performed *wudu* before visiting the sick (Abu Dawud, vol 2, H 3091). This practice is essential when you visit a patient with burns or a patient with immunity problems. Washing hands before and after visiting a patient is very important. If possible, avoid touching the patient if contagious and any hospital equipment including doorknobs and handrails to avoid infection of any kind.

Keep up this practice in public places and public transportation. Visitors should perform *wudu* as soon as they reach home. Avoid using public washrooms if you can, for the sake of good hygiene. *Wudu* five times a day is the best practice for personal hygiene. As Prophet Muhammad (PBUH) has said, "Cleanliness is half the *imaan*."

If you are sick due to flu or any contagious health problem, do not go to masjid or to a friend's place. If you meet someone in this condition, take extra care.

Another interesting *hadith* with reference to your question is Narrated by Sa'd (RA), the Prophet (PBUH) said, "If you hear of an outbreak of plague in a land, do not enter it; but if the plague breaks out in a place while you are in it, do not leave that place." (Ref. Bukhari, vol 1, hadith # 624)

Shifa (Cure)

108. What are the references of *shifa* (cure) in the Qur'an?

A: Surah 17:82 reads, "We send down (stage by stage) in the Qur'an that which is a healing and a mercy to those who believe…." Hence, in reciting and following the message of the Qur'an, there is cure for the body and soul. Prophet Ibrahim (PBUH) attests to this fact in Surah 26:80 when he says, "And when I am ill, it is He who cures me." Other references are Qur'an 9:14, 10:57(58) and 16:69. Try to read *tafseer* (commentary) of the above verses to get the complete meaning.

109. I am told that the doctors give medicine but Allah (SWT) gives *shifa*. What does it mean?

A: *Allah Ta'ala* has revealed *shifa* to us in *Surah Al-Isra* (verse 82) as follows: "We send down in the Qur'an that which is a healing and a mercy to those who believe…." So, the cure is in the hands of Allah (SWT).

Doctors try their best to diagnose and prescribe medical treatment to help cope with disease. Full knowledge of medicine and cure rests with Allah (SWT), as we see sometimes that a certain medicine is given to many patients for a disease or ailment but not every patient gets cured!

I once came across a man who had become blind a few years ago. Even in sickness he looked contented and smiled as he said, "Allah is my doctor and *du'a* is my medicine." Allah awards health and cure to whomever He wishes and to the extent He wishes. We depend on His mercy. May Allah (SWT) bestow His mercy on all of us. *Aameen*.

Dental hygiene

110. **Bad breath during Ramadan is the problem. How can I help myself?**

A: It is a simple matter of dental hygiene. (See details under "Ramadan and fasting.")

111. **If my dentist asks me not to gargle or rinse my mouth for a few hours after the treatment, how should I perform my *wudu*?**

A: Go without rinsing your mouth. Allah (SWT) knows your situation best. (Qur'an 5:6)

Ar-Ruqyah

112. **What is *Ar-Ruqyah*?**

A: One of the practices of *Rasool Allah* and his immediate followers was to recite certain passages of the Qur'an, especially the verses related to *Targheeb* (the rewards) for the sick. This is called *ruqyah*.

The words under a *ruqyah* must be parts of the Qur'an dealing with the names or attributes of Allah.

The practice of *ruqyah* should be absolutely free from any kind of *shirk* (equating another with the authority of Allah). At no point or time, a magician or a soothsayer should be involved in any manner.

Your trust and faith should be only in Allah (SWT), not in *ruqyah*.

Surah Fatiha, *Ayatul-Kursi* and the last three *surahs* of the Qur'an are very effective any time and anywhere.

(Ref. "Health & Healing in the Qur'an," *Islamic Perspectives in Medicine*, by Ahmed Elkadi, MD P 117-122)

113. **Can you give me an example of Prophet Muhammad's practice regarding Ar-Ruqyah?**

A: Ay'isha (RA) has reported that during the fatal illness, the Prophet (PBUH) recited the *Mu'auwidhat*, that is, *Surah An-Nas* and *Surah Al-Falaq*, blew his breath over his hands and rubbed his hands over his body.

When his illness aggravated, she did the same, and rubbed her hands over his body.

Surgery

114. **I wear a gold locket with the inscription of *Ayatul Kursi* on it. I never wanted to part with it at any time, especially when I was being taken for my surgery. The doctor insisted to take it off before the surgery and I had to.**

A: The doctor was right, because during the process of surgery everything has to be very clean and sterilized. Your jewellery could also cause obstruction. If you find tranquility in having an article with the Qur'anic inscription on it, keep it under your pillow. Do not forget to take it back to your home. It is not a bad idea to avoid constantly wearing jewellery with Qur'anic inscriptions, because one goes to washroom with it and handles it when one is not clean enough. Be proud to wear such things during special occasions. In fact, you invoke more blessings from Allah through recitation, contemplation and practicing Islam than you do by the wearing of articles with Qur'anic inscriptions on them.

115. **My surgery is scheduled for next week and I am scared to death about it. Please suggest a suitable *du'a* for me.**

A: Trust in Allah for any kind of problem. Recite, *"Wa ufaw wedo amree illallah, innallaha baseerun bil ibaad"* — "I commit myself to Allah; verily Allah watches over His servant's needs." (Qur'an 40:44)

You may recite: *La ilaha illallah alazeem alhaleem, la ilalha illallah rab alarsh alazeem, la ilalha illallah rab alsamawat wa rab alarad wa rab alarsh alkareem* — "There is no other god except Allah, the magnificent the forbearing. There is no other god except Allah, Lord of the magnificent throne. There is no other god except Allah, Lord of the heavens, Lord of the earth and Lord of the noble throne". (Ref: Bukhari, Muslim, and Ahmed.)

116. **Can you suggest a prayer of thanksgiving after a successful operation?**

A: *Alhamdu lillah allazi bena'amatehe tateem alsalahat* — "All praises are for Allah (SWT) by Whose favour good works are accomplished." Upon receiving any unpleasant news, or even otherwise, say: *Alhamdu lillah Ala kol haal* — "All praises are for Allah (SWT) under all circumstances." (Ref: Al-Hakim and Ibn Al-Sunni.) Regarding *salaat* during surgery, refer to Question # 65.

Baby

117. *Alhamdulillah, Allah Ta'ala* **has blessed me with a baby. What is my first duty as a Muslim when a baby is born?**

A: As soon as the baby is born, at the first opportunity, *azan* is chanted in the right ear and *iqama* in the left ear of the baby. *Aqiqa* (shaving of head) is for boys and girls, which is a *sunnah* of the Prophet. Circumcision for the boys is another *sunnah*.

In some countries, it is customary that a bit of mashed date is place on the baby's tongue. Another practice is to make the baby lick some honey. One has to be careful regarding honey because, sometimes, bees collect pollen from certain flowers to which the baby may be severely allergic.

Insomnia

118. **Sometimes, I wake up in the middle of the night and cannot go back to sleep due to insomnia. Can you suggest a *tasbih*?**

A: Allah Ta'ala has made the day for work and the night for rest (Qur'an 25:47). Recite any *tasbih*. *Afzal-uz-Zikr* (best of the *tasbeeh*) is, *La ilaha illallah* and *Afzalud-Du'a* (best of the *du'a*) is, *Alhamdu-lillah*. Recite *Ayatul-Kursi*, or *Ayat-e-Karima* (*La ilaha Illa anta Subhanaka inni kuntu minazzaalimeen*), or simply a *darood*. You may even wish to imagine the scene of the Kaaba with *tawaf* or certain script from the Qur'an in your mind, and keep concentrating on it while you keep your eyes closed. Take a few deep breaths and mentally order your mind to go to bed. Make yourself the boss here!

If you can afford in your situation, you may even think of simply leaving the bed, sit up, read something interesting and go back to bed when you are sleepy again. If the problem persists, consult your doctor.

119. **Has Prophet Muhammad (PBUH) said anything about insomnia or sleeplessness?**

A: When Zayd bin Thabit complained to the Prophet of his inability to sleep, the Prophet told him to recite: "O Allah, stars have set, eyes have rested, You alone are the Ever-Alive, and the Self-Subsisting Source of all being; neither slumber nor sleep overtakes You. Make my night comforting for me, and bring sleep unto my eyes." Thus Zayd's condition was cured. Sincerity in making *du'a* is important.

On another occasion, when Khalid bin Walid complained about the same condition, Rasool Allah asked him to recite: "O Allah, O You who are the Lord of the seven heavens and whatever they shelter, and the earths and whatever they contain, and You are the Lord of devils and whomsoever they mislead, You be my Guardian-Protector against the evils of all of

Your creatures; guard me against their intrusions and invasions. Noble is the one who enjoys Your protection and Glorified is Your name." Thus Khalid enjoyed restful sleep.

Psychiatric Problems

119. I feel scared in the hospital because of nightmares and bad dreams. What advice can you give me?

A: This could be a medical problem. Consult the doctor first.

Tasbeeh helps a lot: recite *Surah An-Naas, Al-Falaq*, and *Ayatul- Kursi* in the morning and evening. While doing this *zikr* (remembrance of *Allah Ta'ala*), imagine a picture of a page from the Qur'an, and fix your mind on this Qur'anic script and continue *zikr*. You might like to imagine about a scene of *tawaf* at the Kaaba and try to think that you, too, are there and keep reciting *Rabbana aatena fidduniyan hasanah wa fil aakhirati hasana wa qina azaabannaar*. This should, *Insha Allah*, help rid your fears as well as help you gain some virtues. No creation of Allah can harm you until it is the Will of Allah. This is clearly stated in the Qur'an (see Surah 2:102).

120. I feel very hopeless and overcome by despair. I do not feel like doing anything. How can I improve my condition?

A: It is quite common for a sick person to feel depressed. However, one should never lose hope. Allah (SWT) is with those who show and practice patience. Put your whole trust in Allah (SWT). Your family and friends should help to cheer you up. Be content with what you have in terms of health and always think positive. Allah (SWT) is not pleased with those who show ingratitude. (Qur'an 22:38) In *Hadith-e-Qudsi*, Allah says, "My compassion surpasses My anger." (Ref: Muslim and Bukhari). Do not hesitate to discuss this with your doctor at once. For hopeful expectations from Allah, please refer to the Qur'an (10:62-65; 39:53-61; and 94:1-8).

121. Is disease a curse and a punishment by God? If so, how can I get rid of it?

A: Allah (SWT) is *Rahmaan, Raheem, Gaffaar, Shaafi* (the most Benevolent, the most Merciful, One who forgives, and the only One Who can cure) and more. He will not curse or punish His beings for nothing. Disease is not a curse. Anyone could be inflicted with a disease whether innocent or guilty, as we see sometimes a baby suffering with a horrible disease.

We do not know the wisdom and plan of Allah (SWT). Perhaps it is a test for the patient and those around. According to our Prophet (PBUH), there's no disease for which there's no cure. Trust in Allah (SWT). In this connection, an appropriate *du'a* from the Qur'an is *Muwazzidat*, i.e., *Surahs Al-Falaq* and *An-Naas* (113 & 114).

In fact, Prophet Muhammad (PBUH) said Allah gives disease and suffering to wash off some of our sins. We have to practice patience. Also, ponder over *Surah An-Nisa*, ayah 79, which says, "Whatever good happens to thee, is from Allah; but whatever evil happens to thee, is from thyself."

122. Is disease due to *hasad* (jealousy) or curse by other people? If so, how can I avoid or get rid of it?

A: No. Your destiny (*qadr*) is in the hands of Allah (SWT). However, the most appropriate supplication given in the Qur'an is to recite *Surahs* 113 and 114, *An-Naas* and *Al-Falaq*. In case of a medical problem, your doctor is the choice to start with.

123. Are some of the psychotic problems due to *jinns*? What is the solution? Can I visit the shrines of saints to get some help?

A: It is not right to assume these thoughts. If there's any sign of insanity, see your doctor first and then, if necessary, see the psychiatrist. Frequent recitation of *Surahs* 113 and 114 should help. We have a good lesson regarding this subject in *Surah Al-Baqarah* (2:102)

Visiting tombs or shrines to seek the help of *Auliya Allah* is a grave mistake and is nothing but *shirk*. *Shirk* is enjoining someone with Allah. This is unpardonable in the sight of Allah. The wearing of amulets *(ta'wizaat)* or beads for this purpose is also prohibited in Islam.

Qur'anic Psychiatry by El-Hashmi is an informative and interesting book to read.

124. **I am suffering from some very unusual kind of health problems that doctors and medicines are not able to cure. People are suggesting me to see a black magic specialist. I am tempted to see one. What is your opinion?**

A: Getting involved in any kind of magic either for fun or for getting cured is considered *Haraam* and is a satanic act. It is the work of *shaitan* and leads you to nothing but trouble in this world and in the Hereafter. (Ref: 2:102). The glorious Qur'an enjoins us in Surah 7:200 and 23:97 to seek refuge in Allah (SWT) from *Shaitan*. To ward off evil, Prophet Muhammad (PBUH) has practiced and recommended to recite *Surahs Al-Falaq* and *An-Naas* (chapters 113 and 114 of the Qur'an). "And say 'O my Lord! I seek refuge with You from the suggestions of Shaitan'." (Qur'an 23:97)

Stress

125. **I feel very stressed out. My behavior with people has changed and become very annoying. I quite realize it but feel very helpless. Where can I get help to improve my situation?**

A: Stress is a very common problem of modern times. Young or old, everyone is afflicted by it. Reasons vary from person to person, but mainly it has to do with overworking and being dissatisfied with life. However, it is a temporary and circumstantial problem and it is in our hands to relieve it since stress really is a self-inflicted problem.

A believer knows that anything good or bad is from Allah (*Wal qadri khairehi wa sharrihi minAllahi Ta'ala*). Practicing contentment and patience is the key to live a non-stressful life. Always be thankful to Allah (SWT) for the bounties that He has bestowed on us. Look at people around you who are going through worse times than you are. Keep saying *Alhamdulilla* all the time, be it a loss or gain.

There's a lot of professional help available out there. Consult your physician for advice and direction. Talk it over with a sincere friend or a family member. Sort out things in your life and start it all over again. Do not lose hope. Your situation is bound to improve, *insha Allah*.

Allah (SWT) does not burden a soul beyond its scope." (Surah 2:286).

Also, see *Sabr* under AIDS TO HEALING.

126. **I am stressed out to the maximum. I know that I can still depend on Allah to get some comfort. What is my *du'a* now?**

A: *Inni massanya addurru wa anta arham-ur-rahimeen* — "Truly, distress has seized me, and You are the Most Merciful of those that are merciful." (Qur'an, 21: 83)

Wa idha maridt-tu fa huwa yashfi-een… Wa ajalni min wara-thatti jannatin naeem – "Allah created me and it is He Who guides me: Who gives me food and drink. And when I am ill, it is He (Allah), Who cures me. Allah will cause me to die, and then to live (rise again); And Allah, I hope, will forgive me my faults on the Day of Judgment. O my Lord! Bestow wisdom on me, and join me with the righteous: Grant me a truthful report among the later (generations): Make me one of the inheritors of the garden of bliss." (Qur'an 26:78-85)

La ilaha illa anta subhanaka inni kuntu minaz-zalimeen – "There's no other god but You (Allah), glory to You: I was indeed among the wrongdoers." (Qur'an 21:87)

127. The thought of dying has been terrifying me. I want to find peace in myself. What is the best way?

A: The description of a successful man is in Surah 2:2-5. When time comes, we all have to go. Indeed, there's no bargaining. The promise of Allah Ta'ala is, "To those who do good, there's good in this world, and the home in the Hereafter is even better. And excellent indeed is the home of the righteous." (Qur'an 16:30)

Here are some more verses to remember: "No soul can ever die except by Allah's leave and at a term appointed." (Qur'an 3:145)

Death is inevitable (Qur'an 3:185). You've got to live, aspire for a long life to do good things and earn virtues before it is late. It is best to stop worrying and start living.

Remember the *hadith Qudsi* where *Allah Ta'ala* says, "My compassion surpasses My anger." Allah (SWT) is the Most Merciful and the Most Forgiving. In another hadith by Muslim, it says, "None of you should die without having good expectation in Allah." Hence our *du'a* is, "O my Ever and Eternal (God)! I ask for your mercy."

If the thought is too unbearable, seek a practising Muslim doctor for advice.

Some Fancy Problems

*Visit the website http://www.khilafah.com/books/book1.htm
for some interesting topics such as Islamic Verdict on Cloning,
Human Organ Transplantation, Abortion, Test-Tube Babies,
Life-Support Systems, and Life and Death.*

128. Is gender pre-selection allowed in Islam?

A: Islam is a way of life, chosen by Allah for human beings for a safe and pleasant tenure on earth. If gender pre-selection technology should be used to know whether the fetus is male or female for the purpose of selective abortion, then the answer is No. If the information to be obtained is for the health reasons, then consider it favourably. Some diseases such as hemophilia are sex linked. Caution is warranted here.

It is interesting to note that, when Allah (SWT) says no one knows what the womb is carrying, it perhaps says what the baby is growing up to be — not whether it is a boy or a girl!

129. Doctors want me to abort my fetus for health reasons. What has Islam to say about it?

A: Normally, abortion is not allowed after a period of 120 days. It is all right for medical reasons and to save the life of the mother. A good reference book on the subject is *Abortion, Birth Control & Surrogate Parenting: An Islamic Perspective* by Abul Fadl Mohsin Ebrahim. ISBN-0-89259-031-5, American Trust Publication.

130. It is unfortunate that doctors have diagnosed I can no longer conceive. My husband and I are thinking of a surrogate mother. What does Islam say about this?

A: It is not right. Depending on the problem, like abnormal female genital tract, defective sperm production or any such problem, doctors can help you only within their knowledge and means.

During the procedure of surrogating, sperm and ovum is united in vitro and the zygote is implanted in another woman's womb. The subsequent emotional and legal problems could be immense and much more agonizing than not having a baby.

It is best to talk to a sincere Muslim doctor who has sound Islamic knowledge, who honestly understands the exact problem and gives the technical and Islamic opinion. At the same time, refer to Islamic literature yourself. This is a new field and every situation is different and unique. *Allah Ta'ala* bestows whatever child He wants to whomsoever He wishes. (Qur'an 42:49-50)

May I suggest you read Abul Fadl Mohsin Ebrahim's book, *Abortion, Birth Control & Surrogate Parenting: An Islamic Perspective.* ISBN 0-89259-031-5, American Trust Publication.

131. Due to infertility problems, the only way of having children is by artificial insemination. Is it all right according to Islam?

A: Permissible, as long as this is under wedlock between wife and husband. The point to consider here is that since things happen according to the Will of Allah, do we have to intervene everywhere? Allah knows best. (Qur'an 42:50)

For a very interesting research paper, and more details on this subject, I would suggest reading the paper by Dr Hossam E. Fadel, University Hospital in Augusta, Georgia, USA, published in *Journal of the Islamic Medical Association*, Vol. 25, 1993, pages 14-19.

132. What is the Islamic concept of birth control by sterilization for men?

A: Normally, birth control by sterilization is not permitted for economic reasons. *Coitus interruptus* (withdrawal) was the practice during the time of Prophet Muhammad (PBUH). This was not prohibited. Today we have different methods of birth control. *Allah Ta'ala* is Most Merciful. (Qur'an 16:72, 17:31, 24:32)

133. What about euthanasia (mercy killing) in Islam?

A: Islam doesn't permit euthanasia. There's no such thing as a "mercy" killing. This is perhaps the atheistic way of thinking. Muslim *ulema* have given their opinions by *ijtehad*, which is not possible to summarize in this short answer.

A healthy strong person might make his will while he is alive, but he could change his opinion when he is terminally ill or suffering from intense continuous pains.

Euthanasia is considered as suicide / murder – both of which are *haraam*. It is difficult enough to write a living will about euthanasia, and harder still to adhere to it.

In a clinical situation, the doctor's intention should be to alleviate pain and suffering by administering the painkiller so that it does not become a lethal dose.

While suicide is *haraam* in Islam, euthanasia is legal in Holland. Dr Jamal Badawi of Halifax, Canada, has openly opposed euthanasia in his discussions, audiotapes of which are available from the Islamic Society of North America.

Perseverance has tremendous amount of reward in Islam as mentioned in the Qur'an (Surah 2:155-157 and 39:10). I would strongly recommend you to read Dr Faroque Khan's views on this in the *Journal of Islamic Medical Association* of North America. Vol. 15, # 4, Oct. 1983, and the following references from the Qur'an — 2:195; 4:29; 5:32, 35; 6:152; 17:23-25, 31.

People used to talk about "hardship in life." Now the trend is "mercy killing." A few people talk of the "right to die." We need to be careful that the "right to die" does not become a "right to kill."

Blood and Organ Donation

134. Can you tell me something about blood donation please?

A: Standards differ from country to country, society to society and time to time. Red Crescent could differ from Red Cross. Canadian Red Cross Society wants to receive donations from donors who are between 17 and 70 years of age.

If over-aged, then they see whether you had donated blood between 60 and 66 years of age. You must weigh at least 110 pounds. There should be a gap of at least two months between donations. Less than half a litre of blood is drawn at a time.

This constitutes about 10 per cent of your blood volume. This amount seems a lot, but it is quite safe and normal.

Once blood is drawn, the donor is advised to lie down for a few minutes to relax, drink some juice, have a cookie, and get back to one's routine. Under normal conditions, the donor recovers the blood volume within 24 hours although hemoglobin takes 3-4 weeks.

The above regulations for collecting the blood are almost universal. Identification with signature of the donor is required at the time of accepting the donation. Phone in advance to get all the instructions and eligibility. It is recommended to eat a good meal before you donate blood.

135. Does Islam permit donation of organs?

A: There are no clear-cut injunctions in the Qur'an or Hadith concerning organ donations. Such rulings must come from *ijtehad*, which is consent of the *ulema* under the light of Islamic teachings.

Many of the *ulema* (Islamic scholars) have given favourable consent for organ donation from the dead or dying under certain conditions. Life-sustaining major organs cannot be retrieved before death, the definition of death being that the heart should stop functioning, although some insist on brain death. A living person may donate a kidney, blood or bone marrow.

The expression "major organ donation" is a matter of ongoing debate. Medical research and *fiqh* viewpoints were discussed during the fourth session of the Council of Jurists in Jeddah, Saudi Arabia (Feb. 6-11, 1988).

A number of Muslim jurists think the organ donation is permissible for the purpose of treatment or cure of chronic diseases. However, a will of the deceased is essential before the retrieval of any organ from the dead. Immediate family members may also take a decision in this regard.

According to the research conducted by Jaffer Syed, University of Toronto 1996, the practice of *ijtihad* is no longer a major doctrine in the Sunni school of thought; on the other hand, the Shi'a Muslim leadership actively engages in this effort at present.

The highest authority in the Shi'a community, Ayatullah Sayyid Al Khoie, stated the following:

(1) Transplanting an organ of a dead Muslim is not *ja'iz*; in other words, it is not allowed.

If a person gives permission in his will, his will should be honoured. However, if a Muslim's life depends upon such transplant, it is acceptable to do it without a will.

(2) With the consent of a (living) person for the transplanting, the verdicts are as follows:

(a) If the organ is a major one like an eye, hand or leg, such transplant is not permitted. However, if the organ is not major, but just a little flesh or a piece of skin, then it acceptable to do it. In such cases, it is also acceptable to take money in exchange.

(b) It is allowed to give blood for money.

(c) From a non-Muslim's dead body, organ may be transplanted (into a Muslim). The same is true in the case of a *najis* animal's body part (e.g. porcine valve). It will not affect purity of that person. (Ref: *The Tauzeehul Masa'il of the Late Ayatullah Al-Khoei*).

Other information in this regard: In 1995, a *fatwa* from the Muslim Law Council (London, England) sanctioned organ donation.

In 1977, there was a case in Canada when a lady patient was pronounced clinically dead. Organs were not harvested, but then she survived and led a successful life. A complete story of this lady, Ruth Oliver, was reported in *The Globe and Mail* newspaper, Toronto, March 3, 1999.

136. Can a Muslim accept an organ donation?

A: Yes. Jurists have agreed. Syed 1996 notes that, for the sake of saving a life, even porcine heart valve may be used. According to the researcher mentioned above, the Mufti of Egypt Sheikh Muhammad Sayed Tantawi issued a *fatwa* that "allowed transplanting the liver from a clinically dead person to a fatally ill patient." The *mufti* based his ruling on the concept of brain death where the brain and vital organs have stopped functioning even if the heart is still beating. The *mufti*, as well as other leaders in favour of organ donation, state that in the absence of a signed will, it is permissible to obtain donations from the deceased based on authorization from his or her relatives.

The Islamic Religious Council of Singapore allowed kidney transplantation in 1987. With all these facts available to you, the decision is yours.

137. **What is tissue donation; and, can a Muslim donate or receive tissue?**

A: Yes, a Muslim can certainly donate or receive these tissues when needed. The tissues in question here are bones, valves from the heart and corneas from eyes. All these tissues save the agony of pain and suffering of the victims.

138. **What is brain death? Is it allowed to retrieve organs from a Muslim at this stage of brain death?**

A: Brain death is irreversible and is legal death. According to the Canadian Congress of Neurological Sciences, brain death culminates in an etiology excluding potentially reversible conditions. In other words, all brain stem reflexes are absent.

The patient is classified as brain dead when in a deep coma and there's no response in the cranial nerves from stimulation in any part of body and when no movements such as seizures, dyskinesia, decorticate or decerebrate posturing are present. Other symptoms of brain death are the patient is apneic when taken off respirator, and the conditions listed above persist when the patient is reassessed at a suitable interval.

In an interview with Egypt's leading daily, *Al-Akhbar*, the Imam of al-Azhar University (Sunni school), Sheikh Gad Al Haq, implicitly called the procurement from a donor of an organ for transplant a murder until the patient's heart has stopped.

Syed 1996 also reports that recently, physicians and theologians in Jeddah, Saudi Arabia, ruled that the death of the brain indicates the end of one's life. As far as life support for a brain-dead patient is concerned, quite often we're prolonging death than gaining life.

139. What is autopsy? Is autopsy allowed on a Muslim's body?

A: An autopsy is a surgical examination of a dead body for any external and internal causes of death. It helps medical professionals to understand disease and helps in restoring health to the living.

An autopsy may be performed only on a certain part or on the whole body. In case of Alzheimer's disease, the family can ask only for examination of the brain.

In case of a suspicious death, an autopsy is performed on the entire body to determine the cause(s) of death. An autopsy may also determine whether there are hereditary problems and thus help family members through early diagnosis and treatment.

Normally, an autopsy is not performed. The Muslim mindset is not very enthusiastic about autopsies nor does it encourage pilfering from a dead body. Generally, Muslims insist that an autopsy be performed for a good cause with full respect to the deceased's dignity and without any unnecessary mutilation of his body. However, an autopsy cannot be ruled out in the case of foul play or suspicious death when legal, ethical and moral considerations far outweigh any personal considerations.

Visiting Patients

140. Can you suggest a *du'a* for the patient by the visitors?

A: Aisha (RA) narrates that whenever Muhammad (PBUH) visited a patient, or a patient visited him, he invoked Allah to take away the disease. "O Lord of the people! Cure, as You're the One who cures. There's no cure but Yours, a cure that leaves no disease." (Ref. B. Vol. 7 H 579 p. 392)

Prophet Muhammad (PBUH) is reported to have said that when you visit a sick person, get the person to pray for yourself, for the prayer of the sick is like the prayers of the angels, since during an illness, the sick person is safe from committing sins.

If a *du'a* for healing is planned in the congregation, make sure that the patient wants his name said in public.

141. **Do you recommend visiting patients of other faiths, too, since there are great virtues in *iyadat* (visiting the patients)?**

A: Yes, visiting sick patients of other faiths has been the practice of Prophet Muhammad (PBUH) as reported in *Sahih Bukhari* vol. 7, page 380 in the book of patients (*hadith* # 561): Anas (RA) reported that when a Jewish boy who used to serve the Prophet became ill, the Prophet went to pay him a visit."

In the same hadith, Al-Mussiyab (RA) reported that even though Prophet Muhammad's uncle Abu Talib did not accept Islam, he visited his uncle on his deathbed.

A visit to the sick reminds us of our own position and weakness in life. From a king to a beggar, from the strongest to the poorest, any person can fall sick or be infected by bacteria or virus.

Hence, a visit to the sick person teaches us to be humble and to be prepared to help someone.

Life is a journey from which we never return. It is involuntary and compulsory, too. Regardless of his faith, a sick person reminds us that our own final destination is never far.

142. **Can you suggest a *du'a* in time of sickness (a) by the patient, and (b) by the visitor?**

A: (a) By the patient: *Dha'a yadek ala alazi ta'alam men jasadek wa kol Bismillah thalathen, wa kol saba'a marrat A'auzo billah wa kodratehe men shar ma ajed wa uhazer.*

Place your (or patient's) hand at the site of the pain and say, "In the name of Allah" three times, then make *du'a* seven times: "I take refuge in Allah (SWT) and witness His omnipotence from the evil that I feel and am wary of." (Narrated by Ahmed, Muslim and Ibn Majah)

(b) By the visitor: *Ma men abden muslim ya'aod maredhan lem yahdor ajaloh, yakol saba'a marrat: 'Asa'al Allah alazeem, Rab ela'arsh alazeem an yashfeek' ella uffi.*

"Any Muslim who visits a sick person whose prescribed moment of death has not arrived, and makes *du'a* seven times, 'I ask Allah (SWT) the Supreme, Lord of the Magnificent Throne, to cure you, he [the sick person] will be healed." (Narrated by Abu Dawud, and Altirmidzi)

143. **I am a male social service volunteer representing the local mosque. My assignment includes *iyadat-ul-mareed*, to visit the sick in hospital. What if there is a female patient?**

A: Only lady volunteers should visit female patients. In the absence of such arrangements, a male volunteer could carry a visiting card from the mosque describing the name, telephone number and the kind of service offered. Pass on this card to the female patients through the nursing station well in advance. If the patient is in dire need of something, she calls and gets the service. In emergencies or when dealing with elderly patients, go ahead and help in whatever way you can.

In fact, we must encourage our women to become volunteers. A husband-and-wife team is best for this kind of volunteer service.

144. **I am interested in registering with my local hospital as a "Muslim visitor." What would you suggest?**

A: First of all, besides being really serious and capable of serving voluntarily you've to have the time and means to be able to do so. From my own personal experience, it is ideal to have a husband-and-wife team. They should be partially or fully retired from their jobs, enjoy good health and have a car at their disposal.

Acquire good knowledge about Islam from the Qur'an, Hadith and other writings about visiting and counseling patients. You might have to undergo a short training or orientation from the hospital Spiritual Care department. Talk to your doctor and get some general knowledge about infectious and contagious diseases. Be strict in observing the rules of hygiene. Talk to a hospital visitor if available.

Approach the Spiritual Care department of the hospital with an introductory letter from your mosque or its umbrella organization. Once you're registered, follow the hospital rules strictly. Remember that you're now an ambassador of Islam in the hospital and follow Islamic etiquette.

Ideally, a male visitor should visit male patients and a female visitor should visit female patients. You might like to leave a brochure about coping with sickness or about Islam for the patient to read.

145. A Muslim volunteer visited me on behalf of the local *masjid* while I was hospitalized. I felt very good, made *du'a* for this volunteer and for all those connected with that organization. Now that I am healthy, I feel I should join this service and visit the sick. How should I proceed?

A: I am sure you enjoyed the visit of the volunteer. It is a great service. *Hadith-e-Qudsi* records Allah as saying, "I was sick, how come you did not visit Me?" — meaning, when His servant (a fellow Muslim) was sick! This proves the importance of visiting the sick.

To join such an organization, you should contact your local *masjid* for advice. If such a service is nonexistent in your area, get an introductory letter from your *masjid*, contact the hospital authorities, register yourself, get trained, and enroll as a volunteer.

The Social Service, Pastoral Care or Spiritual Care department of every hospital needs volunteers. Hospitals and church organizations provide pastoral care training. By visiting patients, you'll be blessed with great virtues.

146. I was admitted to the hospital in this big city through the emergency. My folks are away from here in a small town. How can they visit me?

A: Most of the hospitals have the facilities to give temporary accommodation to the relatives of the critically ill in-patients. They charge a fee for the hostel, but you get all the conveniences of boarding and lodging including cooking your own meals. Find out about this facility from the hospital authorities.

147. I enjoy visiting patients and I pray for the recovery of the patient. What else can I do?

A: You can ask the patient to pray for you and your family. It makes the patient feel good, and he or she will pray for you humbly and sincerely. Here's the tradition, according to Ibn Maja: "When you go to see a sick person, you should request him to pray for you. For, the sick person's prayer is just like the prayer of an angel."

We should encourage more and more young people to take an interest in such a spiritually rewarding service. A kind word, a loving note, a sympathetic telephone call or a routine visit are all that is required to cure such conditions as stress, loneliness, old age and depression.

148. I am told visiting the sick is a virtuous thing to do. Is there any *hadith* in this connection?

A: According to the following *hadith*, on the Day of Judgment Allah (SWT) will say: "Son of Adam! Why did you not attend on Me when I fell ill? Man will say, 'Lord! Thou art the Sustainer of the whole universe. How could I attend on Thee?' and Allah (SWT) will say, "So-and-so of My servants fell ill, and you did not care for him. Had you paid a visit, you would have found Me!"

Ali (RA) says, "If a man visits a patient in the evening, seventy thousand angels come along with him seeking forgiveness from Allah for him till the morning, and he will have a garden in Paradise." (Abu Dawud, vol 2, Hadith #3092)

In another *hadith*, Anas bin Malik quotes Prophet Muhammad (PBUH) as saying, "If anyone performs *wudu* well and pays a visit to a sick Muslim brother seeking his reward from Allah, he will be removed a distance of sixty years from Hell." (Abu Dawud)

Notice the point of hygiene in the *hadith*!

149. **Is there any special protocol or special needs of seniors that I should be aware before I make a social visit in the palliative care facilities of a retirement home?**

A: The etiquette and protocol described earlier remains the same. For the elder folks in particular, never underestimate or mistake their memories. Never ask them "Do you remember me?"

On the other hand, during your conversation you may somehow reintroduce yourself indirectly. This is because, in the retirement homes, residents come across many visitors and staff. To remember all these occasional visitors by their faces and names is not easy for everyone.

Also, in addressing elderly patients, you need to speak slowly and clearly. If you realize you need to speak a little louder, you should do so without disturbing other patients or involving others in the vicinity. It is possible that the older folks might get confused and not quite follow what you're saying. Take care of the situation humbly and respectfully.

Residents of retirement homes might take a pleasure of taking you to their visitors' lounge to honour you. Do accept. It provides a little change for them to move around and even to show to their co-residents that there are people who care for them.

It's a good idea to remind them tactfully and politely about *ibadaat, tayammum* and to recite the Qur'an regularly. If you don't know what to tell them, talk about some interesting news of the city or from abroad. Do not indulge in any aggressive or heated conversation or disagreement. It's always fun to lose an argument in order to win over the other person, especially an elderly person in need of care.

You may wish to find out what time their food is served, so that you can visit either before or later. This way they will have their regular mealtime company and also enjoy a hot meal at their own pace. A gift of a favourite fruit or cookies can be wonderful. If there is a family picture there, talk about it.

150. **I visit the sick in the hospitals routinely. What should I do when a non-Muslim patient asks me to pray for him (or her) also?**

A: We are all part of God's creation and everyone deserves to be treated well. On humanitarian grounds alone, there's nothing wrong in wishing well for a non-Muslim during their sickness. It is our duty to seek Allah's guidance and pray for good health for one and all.

Our Prophet (PBUH) said: "Whenever you go to see a sick person, you should console him and sympathize with him. Though by so doing you cannot change his fate, you will at least make him happy for a while." (Tirmizi, Ibn Majah)

151. **Can you suggest a *du'a* to be said at the bedside of a patient?**

A: Recite *Surah Fatiha*, since this is also called the *surah* of *shifa*. Advise the patient to recite it himself too. Or, you may say *"Ishfikallah"* which means, May Allah (SWT) heal you. This one word is also a *du'a* by itself.

You will find more *du'as* at the end of the book.

152. **One of my best friends is in the intensive care unit of the hospital. I am not allowed to visit him. What sort of gift can I give him?**

A: The only visitors allowed in the ICU are immediate family or next to kin — one or two of them for a very short time. This is to ensure the patient gets total rest without getting excited or exhausted. The best gift one can give is sincere *du'a*. A get-well card with a few words of *du'a*, hope and encouragement would be fine. Don't send flowers, balloon-a-ramas or food of any kind.

If the patient is at home, you may take some prepared food, but it is advisable to check any dietary restrictions with the family first.

According to Abu Umamah (RA), Prophet Muhammad (PBUH) said, "Treat your sick with charity." Give alms on their behalf!

153. **My best friend is stricken with cancer. How can I help her?**

A: Share some kind words of encouragement to fight back her anxieties along with a sincere *du'a* for a complete healing. There are some excellent books that describe how to cope with cancer, especially during and after chemotherapy. You may buy a book or two about this topic as a gift. A favorite homemade meal would also make a nice gift.

154. **I went to visit to my friend in the hospital, but I found the patient's door closed. I hesitated to get in. What's the best thing to do?**

A: Do not enter the closed door of a patient. Knock gently, identify yourself by name, and inquire if you could visit. Respect the answer. The same etiquette holds good if the curtain is drawn around the bed.

155. **Is there any special etiquette while visiting a patient?**

A: It is important to let the patient talk. Experienced counselors know full well the therapeutic value of listening to the patient. Remember, we have two ears and one mouth, so use them proportionately.

Respect the patient's space. Do not lean upon or sit on the bed, which could be inconvenient to the patient. Stand at a position at which the patient can comfortably see your face.

If the patient is very familiar and if he insists, sit close to him, near the head. Visit the patient only during visiting hours. Acknowledge the other patients in the same room if they see you, and respect their privacy too.

A patient's health condition is his or her privacy. Treat such things as confidential. Any act of kindness and service is a good gesture. Talk in a low voice, and do not indulge in stressful talks, arguments and unpleasant looks. It is not a good idea to suggest another medicine.

156. **I am sick to the extent that sometimes I frown even at my caregivers. I am helpless.**

A: Not all diseases are forever; better days are just ahead. Caregivers are there because they are sincere and understand your misery and they are obliging you. During a long illness or old age, you might become cranky or might even play childish with your own spouse. Be patient, try to be realistic and understand your position. It pays to make *du'a* and co-operate.

157. Some of my friends visit me in the hospital. However, they stay a little too long, which I find rather inconvenient. How can I handle this?

A: This is a matter of etiquette. Rasool Allah (PBUH) has taught us to make short visits to patients. Do not hesitate to tell your visitors if you are sleepy, or like to have some quiet time and rest.

The Prophet's practice was not to prolong his stay with the sick person, nor to raise unnecessary noises near him.

158. Many of my friends visit me in the hospital, which is a great comfort to me. I thank them and pray for their prosperity and Allah's guidance. What has Prophet Muhammad (PBUH) told us about this?

A: Visiting the sick is a great virtue and a *sunna* of the Prophet. We must keep it up and encourage others.

Three very important things that Prophet Muhammad (PBUH) has said in one *hadith* narrated by Abu Musa As-Ashaari (RA) are: "Feed the hungry, visit the sick, and have the captives set free."

159. Is there any sense in visiting an unconscious patient?

A: Bukhari records that, accompanied by Abu Bakr (RA), Prophet Muhammad (PBUH) visited his companion Jabir Bin Abdullah (RA) who was unconscious in a coma.

It is an encouragement and appreciation to the family members and the caregivers who need someone to talk to and to be consoled in time of such distress.

160. Can a person of the opposite sex visit a patient?

A: Only a *mahram* can visit the sick if he/she is alone in the hospital, unless the patient is an elderly person, or you're with your family. In case of an emergency, a second person is preferred. We should not give room for *khalvah*, which is two unrelated persons of the opposite sex to be alone.

Circumstance is a factor here. In fact, *Rasool Allah* (PBUH) visited Umm us-Saib when she was sick, and *sahabiat* (lady companions of the Prophet) attended the thirsty *mujahidin*. (Ref. Muslim)

161. My old uncle is an inpatient in hospital. Can you suggest a gift for him when I go to visit him?

A: Your visit with a smile, and *du'a*, will certainly please your uncle very much. He will make *du'a* for you, which is indeed priceless.

I cannot suggest the most suitable gift as I do not know his special choice, but certainly a small slab of marble (from the ceramic tile shop) or even a piece of onyx work to facilitate *tayammum* will amuse your uncle and remind him of his *salaat*. This is one way of encouraging someone to keep up their *salaat*.

162. When we visit my uncle in the isolation ward, each visitor has to wear a yellow isolation gown and a facemask. He gets scared to see us this way.

A: It is but normal that he should think he is in great trouble. He needs further education, comfort and reassurance that this is a temporary problem.

He is suffering from an infectious disease, so healthcare workers and visitors need to protect themselves from the bugs, which include infectious virus, fungus or bacteria.

Similarly, visitors must wear the yellow isolation gowns, especially if the patient suffers from skin burns in order to protect the patient from any infection from the visitors.

Other Diseases

163. **My father, who suffers from Alzheimer's, is becoming more and more forgetful as time goes on. He was very particular about his religious duties and obligations. Now, he does not know what he's doing. He performs *salaat* frequently in his own time, in his own way. How can I help him?**

A: *Ibadah* (prayers) and other duties are only for adults and sane people. In this case, may Allah (SWT) accept your father's prayers and supplications and reward him generously. This situation is an eye- opening lesson and a warning for us to lead a good life while we are aware of our surroundings.

164. **Recently I had a mild attack of paralysis of my right hand and I partially lost my power of speech. I do not know what it is leading to!**

A: Keep in constant touch with your doctor and follow his instructions. It is not such a bad idea to practice writing with your left hand so that if you cannot use your tongue or your right hand, at least you will be able to write with your left hand to communicate with others. It does not hurt to learn something new. Learning will at least help to keep you pleasantly occupied.

165. **I am hardly in my thirties and, due to a severe case of diabetes, it appears that I am losing my eyesight. I am really scared.**

A: It is indeed very unfortunate. At this stage, do not lose hope of getting cured. Miracles do happen by the grace of Allah (SWT) and there's a remedy for every disease. Moreover, science has made tremendous leaps in combating diabetes.

You might like to spend some time learning Braille so that you are not defeated by your ailing condition. Take it up as a challenge and work towards other avenues; you will be glad!

Also, learning to recite the Qur'an by *tajweed* will lead to a great experience of *sukoon* (tranquility). You may even learn a musical instrument that you like. Such learning keeps you preoccupied and is always an asset.

166. My disease is "old age" for which there's no cure, as Prophet Muhammad (PBUH) has said. What can you suggest to me or to a person suffering from a chronic disease or long-term illness?

A: I am glad you're aware of the Islamic knowledge, and at the same time, you are *sabir* (untiringly patient) and *shakir* (grateful and obliged). In my view, the best thing for you is to be *zakir* (one involved in the remembrance or *zikr* of *Allah Subhanahu wa Ta'ala*). In fact, *Allah Ta'ala* is pleased when a person practices *zikr* privately. This is true *ibada*, a remembrance of the Lord performed with humility and in private, not to be seen by others. (Qur'an 7:55)

This is achieved by involving yourself in reciting the Qur'an, *tasbeeh* or *darood*, especially in the latter part of the night. *Allah Ta'ala* describes Himself as *Sami-ud-dua* (Hearer of the prayers).

167. I suffer from muscular dystrophy. My lungs are badly affected and I have difficulty breathing. As a result, I'm extremely depressed.

A: May Allah (SWT) relieve you from distress and give you *sabr* and courage. By the grace of our Creator, we live in an age when medical science has made tremendous progress. You know that everything is being done to help people like yourself. As Rasool Allah (PBUH) has said, there's a cure for everything. We should not give up hope.

Meanwhile, this is a lesson (*ibrat*) for those who are healthy. Healthy people, better thank Allah (SWT) by saying *Alhamdulillah* each time they inhale, and repeat *Alhamdulillah* when they exhale.

168. **I am a confirmed case of cancer and the doctor has told me that my life expectancy is only about six months. What am I going to do now?**

A: A Muslim believes that death is inevitable; disease is not. Doctors are knowledgeable and they say such things based on experience. They treat and give medicines. *Shifa* (cure) comes from Allah (SWT), and life and death is in His hands. Put all your trust in Allah.

Doctors have also experienced that many patients do not die as per their prognosis. Cancer is not a death sentence anyway. However, refer to the Qur'an (2:45, 3:102, 93:1-5), which teaches us: "Seek help in patience and prayer; and truly it is hard except for the humble-minded."

A *du'a* taught by *Rasool Allah* (PBUH) is: "O Allah, keep me alive as long as life is better for me, and let me die, if death is better for me." (Bukhari, vol 7, #575, p 390)

There are many books that explain in simple language all there is to know about cancer, its treatment and effects on the patient. It is a good idea to read up on cancer and to trust Allah Ta'ala to take you into the folds of His mercy when you're in despair. It is a time of reflection and *astaghfaar*. Give thanks to Allah (SWT) for the good life you have had and pray for better things ahead.

No matter what, we have to fight back the disease till the end. Never forget that Allah is the *Shaafi* (The Healer).

Terminal Health Condition

169. **What should a Muslim do when a serious disease is confirmed?**

A: Being a believer in the *Khaliq* (Creator), one has to submit to the will of Allah. *Du'a* and medical treatment is the next step. This is not the end of the world. After all, as Muhammad (PBUH) has said, Allah has not created a disease without creating a cure for it, except old age. One does not have to give up hope.

The fact of the matter is, if Allah touches you with affliction, none can remove it but He; and if He touches you with happiness, no one can take that away from you. Allah has power over all things. (Qur'an 6:17)

A great *du'a* from the Qur'an is the petition of Yaqub (AS), "Lo! Adversity has afflicted me, and Thou art Most Merciful of all who show mercy." (Qur`an 21:83). Always trust in Allah's power to heal, "And when I am ill, [says Ibraheem (AS)], it is He who cures me." (Qur'an 26:80)

Never take it as a defeat. Let us take an honest look at the two choices open to us:

(a) Be thankful to Allah (SWT) that you did not die a few years ago. You did have chance and still have some time to contemplate. Do whatever good deeds you can accomplish so that Allah Ta'ala may shower His mercy on you.

(b) Consider this notice as a defeat, curse the Creator and your well wishers, weep, cry and feel more pain. This is not the end. You still have to leave this world.

The choice is yours.

170. **My job requires me to be outside the city most of the time. I don't have any relatives to care for my grandfather who has been confined to a long-time care/nursing home due to a terminal illness. I want to leave instructions with the nursing home staff regarding my grandfather's last-minute care in case of death. Can you guide me please?**

A: It is indeed an unfortunate situation. Despite all your efforts, if you or another relative cannot be by your grandfather's bedside at the time of death, request the hospital staff as follows:

When death approaches, ask the hospital to call the Social Service, or Pastoral/Spiritual Care volunteer to arrange a Muslim spiritual caregiver to attend. If not, call the local *masjid* and ask for help. In the nursing home, you make sure to leave names of the persons to approach, their consent, and their updated telephone numbers.

In any case, if death has occurred, the staff should straighten the arms and legs. Tie both the toes, with some gauze, to keep legs together. Alternatively, cross one leg on the other for some time. Close the eyes, keep the mouth closed, by tying the chin (with gauze) around the head.

A member of the same sex, Muslim or Muslima as the case may be, should handle the body. If Muslims are not available, then same sex non-Muslim. If this is not possible, anyone else could perform this duty.

In most big cities, funeral arrangements are available through the local *masjid*. One should inquire, participate and, if possible, be a volunteer in arranging funerals. Serve the community and make friends before you expect someone to help you.

If a dying person is conscious enough, let him/her say *shahada* and *"Allahum ighfarly wa irhamni wa alhekni belrafeek ala'ala"* — "O Allah, forgive me, have mercy upon me, and unite me with the highest companion." (Narrated by Al-Bukhari and Muslim)

171. I am sitting by the bedside of my father in the hospital, who is not expected to live long. Can you enlighten me about how to handle this situation in detail please?

A: Death is inevitable, as the Qur'an has revealed by saying, "Everyone has to taste death." We should have this basic knowledge for ourselves as well as for the sake of others. Keep your will updated and handy. Inform the family, a trusted friend or a relative about the whereabouts of your will.

As the signs of death approach, try to give a feeling of closeness by holding the patient's hand. The dying person should be helped and politely reminded to recite the *Shahada*, that is, "There's no god but Allah, and Muhammad is His messenger." People around can recite *Surah Yaa-Seen*, the 36th chapter of the Qur'an. Ask for Allah's mercy and forgiveness for the dying person. It is a good practice to help the dying person perform *wudu* with a wet towel. Some Muslims like to turn the face of the patient towards Makkah. It is not mandatory to do this.

After death has occurred, eyes are closed, and mouth is closed (with the help of a bandage, running around the chin and head). Arms and legs are straightened. The big toes are tied together to keep the legs together.

While closing the eyes of the dead, recite, "O Allah! Make his affair light for him, and render easy what he is going to face after this, and bless him with Your vision, and make his new abode better for him than the one he has left behind."

Any local *masjid* with funeral services may be approached for further help in bathing, shrouding, *salat-us-janaza* (funeral prayer) and burial.

If the question of organ donation crops up, look for the will or consult the closest relatives and decide. Autopsy is discouraged. Cremation is out of the questions and burial should not be delayed unnecessarily.

172. **What can be a *du'a* by the patient himself before death if he is still conscious?**

A: The dying person is politely reminded to recite:

"La illaha illah wa Allah akbar, la illah illah wahdah, la illah illah wahdah la shareeklah, la illah illah laho almolk wa laho alhamed, la illah illah wa lahawl wa la kowah illa billah" — "None has the right to be worshipped except Allah, and Allah is the Greatest. None has the right to be worshipped except Allah, alone. None has the right to be worshipped except Allah, Alone without partner. None has the right to be worshipped except Allah, to Him belongs all sovereignty and praise. None has the right to be worshipped except Allah, and there is no might and no power except with Allah." (Ref: Altirmidzi and Ibn-Majah)

"Allahum ighfairle wa irhamni wa alhekni belrafeek ala'ala" — "O Allah, forgive me, have mercy upon me, and unite me with the highest companion". (Ref: Bukhari and Muslim)

173. **My father is in hospital and the doctor has given up hope, saying it is a matter of one or two days at most. At this time, the doctor has started giving painkiller and sleeping drug (morphine) through IV (intravenous). My father is not able to think and cannot express his feelings and thoughts, nor is he able to convey his last-minute wishes or any advice to me, nor listen to us when we whisper and remind him *Shahada* in his ears.**

A: Such drugs are given to the patients at the time described above, to reduce the pain and suffering in the final hours of life. Under the Health Care Consent Act (Ontario, Canada, 1996), the attorney, spouse, nearest relative or even the friends can consult and request the doctor to discontinue such a drug for a period of time.

The patient may regain conscience, may be able to think, express and listen. By doing so, the patient could go through the agony of pains. It is best perhaps to consult the patient at this stage whether to continue such a drug or to leave him alone. Respect the wishes of the patient at all times. Not too long ago, the author personally came across this kind of a situation where he saw the patient recover and got back to normal. We cannot come in the way of Allah's decisions!

174. Unfortunately, my wife delivered a stillbirth. What am I going to do for the funeral?

A: In case of stillbirth, the fetus is shrouded and buried. Funeral directors need the name of baby/fetus. *Ghusl* is not necessary. No *salat-uz-janaza* is conducted. Friends provide comfort for the family. If the baby had breathed even for a few seconds and then died, the baby has to be named and all funeral rites are to be observed.

175. Is there a *du'a* for a stillbirth or for a child's death?

A: After seeking forgiveness for the deceased, recite, *"Allahom ega'alaho fartaan wa zokhraan le-waledaih, wa shafei'an mojabaan. Allahom thakeel behe mawazenahoma, wa a'azeem behe ugorahoma, wa alhekoho besaleh almu'mineen. Wa ija'alaho fe kafalat Ibrahem wa kehe berahmatik azab aljaheem"* –

"O Allah, make him a preceding reward and a stored treasure for his parents, and please accept his pleading. O Allah, through him, increase his parents' reward. Unite him with the righteous believers, place him under the care of Ibrahim (PBUH), and protect him by Your mercy from the torment of hell."

176. What is the next step to be taken once the patient is dead?

A: On noticing or hearing about death, Muslims say: *"inna lillah wa inna ilaihi raaji-uun"* — "To Allah we belong and unto Him is our return." (Qur'an)

The family of the deceased should recite: *"inna lillah wa inna ilaihi raaji-uun, Allahum ajeerni fe musebati wa ukhloof li khairan menha"*—

"To Allah we belong and unto Him is our return. O Allah, compensate me for my hardship and replace it for me with something better." (Ref: Muslim)

Family and friends are encouraged to recite *Surah Yaa-Seen* (Chapter 36). When closing the eyes of the deceased, they should say,

"Allahom ighfer lefolan (beismoh), wa irfa'a daragatoh fe almahdee'in, wa ikhlofeh fe akebeh fe alghabereen, wa ighfer lana wa lah ya rab alalameen, wa afseh lah fe kabreh, wa nower lah feeh" —

"O Allah, forgive [name of the deceased] and raise his rank among the rightly guided … and those he has left behind, and forgive us and him, O Lord of the worlds. Make his grave spacious and illuminate it for him." (Ref: Muslim)

Once death is confirmed, doctors will release the body. It might be necessary, in certain circumstances, for the hospital authorities to await a post-mortem examination or a pathologist's report. If you explain to the authorities about the early burial tradition in Islam, the hospital will try to facilitate early release of the body. A death certificate is issued by the hospital for other uses. For the burial, the undertakers would ask some details about the deceased.

Loneliness and Palliative Care

177. I am getting old and weak. I don't know what is next!

A: For an easy life it's a good idea to keep your love of worldly goods and material luxuries well in check. Be content and thankful to Allah, as well as to all those people who care for you and come in contact with you. Always make *du'a* for the service you are getting.

It is always nice to thank Allah for giving a long life and good conscience. Say, "*Ya Allah*, as I am advancing in my age and becoming weaker, make my life easy and make me closer to You." It's up to you to keep it up.

178. **Loneliness is my problem. How can I help myself, and who can help me?**

A: No one is really alone. Loneliness is only an attitude. *Allah Subhanahu wa Ta'ala* is closer to us than our jugular vein. He hears when we call Him. Allah (SWT) is omnipotent and He watches over us all the time. He is ever-present and always there even before we call Him. His word is the Qur'an, and this Book is everlasting. To read the Qur'an is to speak to Allah (SWT). To stand in *salaat* is to face Allah (SWT). If you cannot see Him during *salaat*, then imagine that He is seeing you. In fact, the position of *jalsa* during the *salaat*, when we recite *Tashahhud*, is indeed the *miraj* (meeting with *Allah Ta'ala*) of the *musalli* with the *Khaliq* (Creator).

It is not right for a Muslim to think he or she is ever alone. Recite the Qur'an in a slow rhythm at any time, anywhere, in a wholehearted and sincere manner. You will feel you're in fact talking to Allah (SWT). Tears of joy may roll down your cheeks and you will never feel alone – or lonely. Your cry will be heard and answered, *Insha Allah*.

If you cannot read the Qur'an, play a tape recited by a *qari* and then listen carefully. Ponder over it, read the translation if possible. In fact, it is a never-ending business to read about the interesting Islamic history and stories of the *Sahaba*. You should always look forward to go to *masjid* for *salaat*, at least for the Friday congregational prayers and to meet other Muslims. Never think you are alone or isolated. Talk to someone and make friends. Keep in contact with your relatives and renew your relationship.

If you've grandchildren, you can really enjoy their company but do not intrude much in their parent's privacy. People, including your own children, resent such intrusion.

Remember that marriage is a must for a Muslim. Remarry if you so desire! There might be a person like you out there somewhere with a similar predicament.

According to Prophet Muhammad (PBUH), acquire knowledge, which will be useful while you are lonely. Call your local *masjid*, ask for information about Muslim social organizations. Go out and work as a volunteer in a hospital, or perhaps do some maintenance work for your *masjid!* Help your neighbour, help in the children's school nearby, and get involved. These things could be rather difficult to start with, but it will soon become an interesting routine and be very rewarding. Use your past skills.

Buy a pet, teach some tricks and learn your own lessons. Indulge in physical exercise along with it. Be happy and healthy. Have you ever listened to music from different parts of the world? It is interesting. You may borrow audio taped music from your public library – just remember that not all kinds of music is considered all right in Islam.

People are lonely because they build walls around themselves instead of building bridges. If you're old and weak, accept the fact honorably and not as a defeat. You did enjoy a long life. Thank Allah *Ta'ala* for all His favors so far and aspire for more.

Ask masjid authorities to introduce you to folks of your position. Befriend those who are lonely.

The government also provides some services for lonely people. Your local "Distress Centre" managed by the city's social services is listed in the telephone book. Look for such things in your city directory. For example,

United Way has a 24-hour hotline service for lonely people or anyone who feels like talking. Their number is (905) 278-7208 in Canada.

Besides, one can always keep busy with unlimited and interesting knowledge available on the Internet, e.g., www.utoronto.ca/seniors.

An interesting website for Islamic books, audios, videos and software is: http://astrolabe.muslimsonline.com.

179. What is palliative care?

A: The World Health Organization has defined palliative care as "the active total care of patients when their disease is no longer responsive to curative treatment and when control of pain, of other symptoms and of psychological, social and spiritual problems is paramount. The overall goal of palliative care is the highest possible quality of life for the patient and family. Palliative care affirms life and regards dying as a normal process.

"Palliative care emphasizes relief from pain and other distressing symptoms. It integrates the physical, psychological and spiritual aspects of patient care, offers a support system to help the patient live as actively as possible until death and a support system to help the family cope during the patient's illness and in bereavement."

180. What information is available about care of parents and elders in Islam?

A: The Qur'an (17:23) tells us, "Your Lord has decreed that you worship none but Him, and that you show kindness to parents. Whether one or both of them attain old age with you, say not to them one word of contempt, nor repel them, but address them in terms of honour."

"... give thanks to Me and to your parents" (Qur'an 31:14)

Directly mentioning parents in the same line with God shows the importance of parents in their old age. According to a famous *hadith*, Prophet Muhammad (PBUH) has said, "Paradise lies under the feet of mother; and to acquire the pleasure of your father is to acquire the pleasure of Allah."

Also, the Prophet has said that if your parents are not alive, and if you wish to accumulate the virtues of serving your parents, serve the brothers and sisters of your parents!

Gentle words and deeds are good medicine for the older folks. Check the Qur'an 17:24, where *Allah Ta'ala* (SWT) asks us to submit to parents with all humility through mercy and say, "My Lord! Bestow on them Your mercy as they brought me up when I was small," and many other injunctions and *hadiths*. Do not wait for the calendar-ordained "Father's Day," "Mother's Day" or "International Year for the Elderlies" to be decreed by the United Nations!

Islamic Organizations

181. **I want to wear an appropriate bracelet indicating that I am a Muslim. This is in case I am found unconscious without any identification. Is there any such thing?**

A: This is an extremely important point. I am not aware of such an organization or a Muslim community registry. However, I hope and wish such things develop and a wide circulation of information is made available. It is time to do something through our major organizations especially in non-Muslim countries.

A number of our folks who retire think that it is time for them to sit down within four walls to wait for their end. No, it is time for opening the next chapter of life with all the acquired contacts and experience. This would be ideal time for social services and to pay back something to your community.

When a patient is brought into the hospital, the admitting clerk asks the name of your religion, faith or church and records it. This information is essential to pass on to the respective clergies or volunteers who could visit their community members and to serve the patient in case of emergencies by providing spiritual care.

If the admission is through emergency, make sure they insert this information in your hospital chart later. The hospitals also keep a record of the masjids, Muslim spiritual caregivers and pastoral care workers. This is done through the social services departments. Your duty as a patient is to tell them at the time of admission that you're a Muslim.

It is not a bad idea to carry a personal identity card or information in your wallet saying you are a Muslim. You may also include contact names and their telephone numbers.

182. Is there any Muslim organization that can come to the rescue of a patient who has no close relatives or friends nearby?

A: In North America, all hospitals have a pastoral care or spiritual care department under their social-services umbrella. Contact them; they are very helpful and will guide you to the local *masjid* for this information. In major cities throughout North America, patient visitation programs organized by the local mosques are common.

183. Is there a Muslim organization that can act on behalf of a Muslim patient without next of kin to give consent to the doctor for special treatment or surgery?

A: Most hospitals have a board of ethics. Under emergency situations, this board decides what to do. Normally, they contact a Muslim organization through the social service organizer. Most importantly, the patient or his family should inform the hospital that the patient wishes to be governed by Islamic jurisprudence. Consent to treatment is a law in many countries.

For details, consult your local *masjid* and your lawyer, well in advance. This is indeed important and urgent.

184. **Can I leave telephone numbers of the *masjid* with my doctor in the hospital for any emergency concerning me?**

A: It is a good idea, but check with your *masjid* or any Muslim social service group in advance. You might be advised of a better or more appropriate place.

185. **Is there any Muslim organization for cancer patients?**

A: Many enthusiastic Muslims started organizing with all the sincerity. They are working hard and need support. Try your local masjid for help and check the Internet for religious websites.

Suicide

186. **Do you think there is a cure for my disease?**

A: Yes. According to the traditions of Prophet Muhammad (PBUH), we know there's a cure for every disease except old age. One should not give up hope. Trust in Allah (SWT); he is the most merciful and beneficent. Please note that there are always pious people who are asking *du'a* for others (like you) whom they do not even know. At least, we know that not all modern medicines can cure diseases, but they certainly help to cope with pain. ·

This much is sure: *Allah Ta'ala* has given you time and consciousness to ask for *astaghfaar* and *hidaya*. It is nice to spend time in contemplation if you can. Never think of euthanasia. This is *haraam*. (Qur'an 2:286, 4:29)

187. **How much *sabr* (patience) should I have for my suffering of the disease?**

A: In a *hadith* narrated by Ibn Abbas (RA), Prophet Muhammad (PBUH) went to visit a sick Bedouin. Whenever the Prophet visited the sick, he would say to them, "Do not worry, it will be expiation [for your sins]," meaning, washing away of your sins. The Bedouin said, "You say expiation? No, it is but a fever that is boiling or harassing an old man, and will lead him to his grave without his will." Prophet Muhammad (PBUH) said, "Then, yes, it is so." (Ref. Bukhari. Vol. 7, p 380 Hadith 560)

This is a good lesson of attitude if one is interested in improving oneself.

188. My pains are so severe that at times I wish I were dead and free from this problem [suicide]. Any advice?

A: Refer to the following *hadith*. Anas bin Malik (RA) reports the prophet of Allah (PBUH) as saying, "None of you should wish for death because of a calamity befalling him; but if he has to wish for death, he must say: 'O Allah! Keep me alive as long as life is better for me, and let me die if death is better for me.'"

Consider the following *hadith*: "The secret *sadaqa* (charity) extinguishes the Lord's anger; preserving the ties of kinship increases the life span; and rendering good to people protects from evil fatalities."

"Make use of medical treatment, for Allah (SWT) has not made a disease without appointing a remedy for it, with the exception of one disease, namely old age." (Abu Dawud, vol 3, hadith #3846)

A Muslim is not afraid of death; he remembers it throughout his lifetime. Death is inevitable and naturally the end of life on earth and time to meet the Lord, which a Muslim looks forward to. Death is only a transfer from here to the Hereafter. In fact, when a Muslim stands for *salaat*, he thanks Allah for giving one more chance to perform *sajda*. One should never commit suicide; it is a sinful act. (Qur'an 2:286, 4:29)

189. I feel depressed and find no interest in life. How can I help myself?

A: With the symptoms you have, it is essential to talk it over with your spouse or family and friends. Do not let things ride: talk to your doctor in the first instance. If the doctor takes it easy, see another doctor because this is not a matter you should take lightly. Treat it with some seriousness.

If you are a mother and feel that you are not a worthy mother for your children, or you want to be away from your child, go to the doctor immediately since it is a most serious health condition. You may be suffering from post-partum depression, which is rather serious but can be cured.

Will

190. Do you think I should write a will before I go for my major surgery next week?

A: Writing one's will is mandatory in Islam since it is mentioned in the Qur'an (2:180, 2:240, 4:4-14, 19, 33, 176-7 and 5:106). Timings of life and death are in the hands of Allah (SWT) only.

Also, Prophet Muhammad (PBUH) has recommended that two nights should not pass without writing a will by the person for his (or her) belongings. Once you've written the will and attested it, including names of the executors, let one or two people know where exactly you keep the will.

Islamic Medicine

191. What kind of information is available under Islamic Medicine?

A: There's a great deal of information about this subject but it's beyond our scope to elaborate on it in this tiny work. Prophet Muhammad (PBUH) has put the Qur'anic information about medicine into practice and taught us enough wisdom. The Prophet's way of traditional, conventional and spiritual medicine is described in many books and on Internet websites. Read Islamic history books.

There's a very emphatic mention in the Qur'an (16:69) about honey as a medicine. Verse 82 of Surah 17 reads, "And We reveal of the Qur'an that which is a healing and a mercy for believers."

Apart from medicines like honey and Qur'anic recitation (Qur'an 17:82), Prophet Muhammad (PBUH) has described very interesting home treatments using honey, herbs, black seed, barley, cow's milk, henna and *miswak*.

The book *Tibb-e-Nabavi* (*Medicine of the Prophet*) by Imam Ibn Qayyim Al-Jawziyya (translated by Muhammad Al-Akili) contains a fairly comprehensive sampling. Also, a large part of Bukhari's Vol. 7 deals with this subject under the heading *Kitab-ul-tibb* (*The Book of Medicine*).

Health Acts, General & Canadian

192. **What is the Consent to Treatment Act in the health care system in Canada?**

A: The Consent to Treatment Act is now the Health Care Consent Act, 1996, which is the law in Ontario. A Ministry of Health publication (Ontario, March 96) says, "Like the repealed Consent to Treatment Act, 1996, deals comprehensively with the issues of consent to health services. The Act clearly establishes the right of people in Ontario to make informed decisions about health treatment. The Act codifies all the elements of consent to health services in one piece of legislation, and applies to treatment provided in all settings by health practitioners specified in the Act.

"The Act also provides a mechanism to obtain a treatment decision from a substitute decision maker for those who, at the time health treatment is required, are not mentally capable of consenting on their own behalf. As a safeguard, the legislation gives people the right to have a finding of mental incapacity reviewed."

In places other than Ontario, please call the respective health care systems, take action and be aware.

193. **Where can I get Canadian government publications and related information, including Consent to Treatment and the Health Care Consent Act, 1996?**

A: For government publications, you should contact: Publications Ontario, 880 Bay Street, Toronto ON M7A 1N8 Tel (416) 326-5300 Toll-free 1-800-668-9938

194. **What is power of attorney and what is power of attorney for personal care?**

A: Power of attorney is the authority by which a person appoints someone he trusts in advance to make decisions for him if he becomes unable to make decisions for himself. The person you appoint is known as your Power of Attorney.

Similarly, the power of attorney for personal care is a legal document by which a person gives legal authority to someone they trust to make personal-care decisions if they become mentally incapable. Personal care includes health care, shelter, clothing, nutrition, hygiene and safety.

A power of attorney for personal care may also contain instructions about how the grantor would like decisions made on his or her behalf. The law requires attorneys to follow those instructions whenever possible. It is important to note, however, that a family member can make health care decisions even when he (or she) does not have the power of attorney for personal care.

Keep yourself informed about the laws of the land or state in which you reside because a law can change at any time. Ignorance of the law is not an excuse. In the United States, for instance, some laws differ from state to state; and, in Canada, from province to province.

195. If I don't have the power of attorney, will I need one to keep the government out of my affairs?

A: Even if you don't have the power of attorney, it is unlikely the government would ever need to be involved. Changes to the law will ensure that family members and friends have priority over the government as a substitute decision-maker.

The Public Guardian and Trustee will only make decisions for people who have no one else to do so. However, it is a good idea to appoint someone you know and trust to make decisions on your behalf if you become incapable. Then your substitute decision-maker is the person of your choice. (Ref: *In Ontario*, a publication of the Office of the Public Guardian and Trustee, March 1996)

196. Under what circumstances is emergency treatment given without consent?

A: Emergency treatment is given without consent to an incapable person. According to the Consent to Treatment Act, the health practitioner has to determine that there's an emergency and any delay in getting a substitute decision would prolong the person's suffering or put the person at risk of sustaining serious bodily harm.

The Health Care Consent Act adds another situation where emergency treatment is given without consent. This is where a person is apparently capable but the communication needed to get an informed consent cannot take place because of a language barrier or disability and there's no reason to believe the person does not wish to be treated.

197. **How is power of attorney different than a living will under the health care system?**

A: A living will is one way of expressing advance directives. Advance directives in any form give substitute decision-makers instructions on the kind of medical treatment or personal care that a patient would wish to be given in any particular situation. A power of attorney for personal care names someone to make decisions for the person, should he or she become incapable. A power of attorney for personal care may also include advance directives.

198. **The Consent to Treatment Act helps the sane adults. Who can help the mentally disabled patients?**

A: In Ontario, the Ministry of the Attorney General looks after the interest of mentally incapable patients, and health practitioners of psychiatric facilities take care of any problems in this connection.

Miscellaneous

199. **My cry is "Why me, O Lord? What did I do wrong for this unbearable pain?"**

A: During his days, Prophet Ayyub (AS) suffered a great deal more than anyone else. All that he said was, "Verily, distress has seized me, and You are the Most Merciful of all those who show mercy." Ayyub, known to our Christian friends as Job, practised *sabr* and *shukr* and was not only healed but also earned his reward in this world and in the Hereafter. (Qur'an 21:83)

Generally, ungratefulness enters our minds through Shaitan's mischief. By reciting, *"Aauzu billahi minash Shaitaan nir rajeem"* you get away from the influence of *Shaitaan*. Our misfortunes are a test for us from Allah. *Sabr* is the answer.

200. I have great difficulty bending my knees to squat while urinating, yet I was taught it's "un-Islamic" to urinate in a standing position. How can I help myself?

A: If it is not possible for you, there's no other way. Thank Allah (SWT) that there are no other serious problems. Hudhaifa (RA) narrates an incident where once the Prophet (PBUH) passed urine near a dump area in a standing position. (Bukhari Vol. 1, Hadith # 224, P 144)

Studies have shown that urinating in standing position results in loss of body protein (tiny amounts, of course) in young men. This condition is termed *orthostaticproteinurea*. (Ref: *Fundamentals of Clinical Chemistry*, 18th edition, N. W. Tietz (ed.), Saunders Co., 1976 page 357)

201. In many countries in the East, the doctor may not tell the patient about the seriousness of the disease. That information is given only to an immediate family member. In the West, however, doctors speak frankly and openly to the patient about the seriousness of the disease and life expectancy. How can I handle this situation regarding my grandmother who is going into hospital in connection with a serious problem?

A: Talk to the doctor in advance. Doctors do respect the values of cultures and religions. In fact they're taught so as part of their training. In Western medical ethics, a physician's responsibility and contract is primarily with the patient. The physician is obliged to tell the facts to the patient. The family is therefore encouraged to cooperate with the physician.

202. My mother does not speak English. She is going to be admitted into the hospital where only English is spoken. How can I arrange for a translator?

A: All hospitals try their best to enlist interpreters. They also usually have printed charts containing pictures of routinely needed things, e.g., picture of bed pan, glass of water, a dinner plate, fruits and so on, which nursing staff may use to understand the needs of patients.

It is a good idea, however, to leave your own or someone else's telephone number next to the patient's bedside phone for hospital staff to dial for help. You may even write in transliteration a few phrases near the bed.

203. **I am a lady, just arrived in this country. I could not find a lady doctor for my medical checkups. Till I get one, can I keep seeing a male doctor?**

A: It is a question of *taqwa* and *dharoora* (piety and dire necessity). It is acceptable since you're helpless at present, and you need medical attention now. But keep working hard and trust in Allah (SWT) and make *du'a* for better arrangements.

Ideally, in order of preference, a *Muslima* (Muslim lady) patient has to see a *Muslima* doctor. If not available, a non-Muslim lady doctor can attend. In her absence, a Muslim male doctor is your best choice.

If that isn't possible, a *Muslima* may visit a non-Muslim male doctor, preferably accompanied by the patient's husband, a lady relative, or a *mahram* male relative to be present at the time of the lady's examination or treatment.

A good rule of thumb is that "the same sex" takes precedence over "the same religion." The same goes for male Muslim patients in need of medical attention.

204. **I consider other patients in my hospital room as my neighbours? How do I help them?**

A: First and foremost, respect their privacy. Speak gently with your visitors or while talking on the phone and be careful that your pungent or spicy homemade meals don't offend their sensibilities.

Be prompt in relaying any messages you receive on their behalf verbally or by phone. Ask whether he or she needs any help within your means.

Also, ensure you don't annoy other users by splashing water around the sink and floor while making *wudu*. Wipe the floor and the sink dry before you leave, otherwise the next person may say, "This (Muslim) patient makes mess in the washroom five times a day!"

Try to tolerate small inconveniences due to the illness or even the innocent unpleasant manners. At the same time, remember that you have your rights, too. Talk to the nurse if necessary. Perform your *salaat* in silence, especially during the *fajr*, when other patients are sleeping in the same room.

Such considerations are part and parcel of basic etiquette.

205. In sharing the room with another patient in a semi-private ward, I have great difficulty coping up with the loud snoring of the other patient. Also, I don't like the blinds opened in the room when I sleep in the afternoons. I do not have much of a choice. Can you give me some suggestions?

A: Nothing much can be done for the other's loud snoring except plugging your ears with cotton wool or with those soft silicone plugs available in drug stores meant for swimmers. As for avoiding bright light during your sleeping time, you may like to cover your eyes with a simple eye-pad available in travel stores.

206. What are some of the interesting developments in medical ethics today?

A: With the advent of wireless healthcare technology, many of today's developments may soon become obsolete. Everyday, there's something new in the field of medicine. Daily, newspapers publish new discoveries and developments.

Radio, television and health journals are other sources. From time to time, the *Journal of Islamic Medical Association* of the United States publishes scientific articles with reference to Islam.

You should visit a hospital or medical library, or browse through the latest journals in your local library. Also, the Internet offers an enormous amount of literature and numerous websites dealing with medical ethics.

207. How do you see medical practices of the future?

A: They'll be amazing, incredible and astonishing. Not only mind-boggling but also mind-blowing!

For instance, pigs have been impregnated with human genes and monkeys with jellyfish genome in order to harvest heart and other body parts for transplantation and disease control studies.

Scientists believe this kind of xenotransplantation (animal organs to humans) will eliminate the problems associated with organ rejection. Such manipulation of genes and DNA is very common today.

Of course, this will add a new dimension to the area of medical ethics but more and more open surgeries will be replaced by endoscopies and remote-controlled robotic operations even when the patient is in a different country!

Diagnoses of problems of internal organs with endoscopes are already a routine thing, and tele-psychiatry is becoming very common. For example, a patient is seen and treated by the psychiatrist through TV monitors away from the doctor's office. This could be from another country to the patient sitting in his own home-town office.

Cancerous tumors could literally be frozen at site or starved to death by squeezing the blood supply or by an immune system trained to kill cancer cells. Experiments are being conducted to introduce certain viruses into the patient's system to attack and destroy only cancer cells; and tremendous improvements have been made in chemotherapy.

In the case of kidney stones, the water content is virtually dried out from the stone and the stone is crushed to powder by laser and eliminated from the system.

The effectiveness of thousands of drugs can be checked instantly on a little card that carries a patient's genetic code. As a result of stricter anti-smoking by-laws, better eating habits, physical exercises and the advances of medical science, life expectancy is predicted to go up by another ten years.

Here's some good news for diabetic patients: Soon they will be getting their insulin hormone by way of an inhaler instead of injection.

At present, heart and kidney operations are done on fetus while it is still developing in womb!

208. **What is your prognosis about acupuncture?**

A: Acupuncture is a method of treating various conditions by pricking the skin with needles. Developed and practiced in China over 5,000 years ago, its benefits are obvious yet it is not fully acknowledged in the West. However, Canada recognizes acupuncture as an alternative medicine and has a growing number of practitioners. In the year 2000, Toronto's Mount Sinai became the first hospital in North America to acknowledge and introduce acupuncture.

209. **I understand that insulin for diabetic patients is extracted from pig's pancreas. Can I take it?**

A: Insulin is also extracted from cows. Your doctor can prescribe the one you ask for. Until the right medicine is available, keep using the one in hand. Do not give up the search for beef insulin.

Scientists have come up with Humulin. This synthetic product acts exactly like insulin and is prescribed by many doctors. Commonly available, Humulin contains no animal products and is safe to take.

210. I don't feel comfortable about the beef insulin prescribed for me because it's not from *zabeha (halaal)* cows. But I am helpless for the sake of my life.

A: You're right, but you don't have to split hairs. *Allah Ta'ala* is more merciful and forgiving than you or I can imagine.

Until facilities are available for such considerations, we must go with what's available. Muslim countries and scientists should address such issues by working on such projects.

211. I seem to be developing diabetes and also have slightly high blood pressure. It is very hard for me to give up my love for sweets. Can you give me some tips?

A: Writing in the April 1986 issue of *Islamic Horizons*, Dr Shahid Athar notes, "Fresh fruits are low in calories and high in vitamin, mineral and fiber content compared to cane sugar. Fruits contain fructose, not sucrose (as in sugar). Fructose has been found to cause no rise in blood sugar; rather it was found to lower the high blood pressure of diabetics." Honey has mostly fructose and is the best.

212. Do you consider tobacco-smoking *haraam*?

A: Some learned Muslim scientists have described and proved it as unlawful. Refer to Dr Ibrahim B. Syed's article in *Journal of Islamic Medical Association*, Vol 15, No 4, Oct. 1983, pp. 110-112, "Smoking is Unlawful in Islam." Besides, there's unanimous universal conclusion by researchers that smoking is deadly.

213. **As a patient in the radiology department, I don't have much choice. Can you give me some idea about the dangerous levels of exposure to the X-rays, ultrasound, CAT scan, and the chest, bone and the gastrointestinal X-rays?**

A: Thank Allah (SWT) we live in an age of tremendous medical and scientific breakthroughs. The radiation equipment used today is quite sophisticated and it should not concern you at all. There are enough regulations in radiology to safeguard you in developed countries.

214. **Now that I'm confined to my hospital bed, I've a small confession to make. My parents tried to bring me up as a Muslim with whatever knowledge and faith they had. In my youth, with the company I had and the world I lived in, no one talked about God. My sickness now is trying to open my eyes about the reality. I know there's something Most Powerful governing the universe. How do you suggest I proceed in search of truth? I don't know where to begin.**

A: *Alhamdulillah*, you are on the right track now. Disease is a test and guidance to those who seek it. We've a physical body and a soul. Body and soul are together during life on earth. They need food and care for their survival.

When the body gets sick, a doctor can help; and when the soul is sick, it has to be nourished with piety, otherwise it goes astray. Allah (SWT) has given us the signs to come back to the right path. One such way is through disease. This is what you're experiencing at this time.

Repentance, what we call *taubah*, is the beginning of a new life. Besides, it is good to keep the company of the righteous all the time. Read, talk and practice Islam, since Islam is "the way of life." Do your best and trust in Allah (SWT) to guide you. Your realization at this point is the beginning. You remember *Allah Ta'ala*, and He will remember you. (Qur'an 2:152)

215. **I am a good person. I wouldn't wish a disease like mine to strike even my worst enemy. How come Allah (SWT) has given this trouble to me?**

A: Most of us are in the same boat as you, and rare indeed is the person who has no problems at all. We tend to forget what the Qur'an tells us: "Everything good to you is from God, anything bad is from your action." (Qur'an 4:79) In another verse, *Allah Ta'ala* says, "Do men imagine that they will be left (at ease) because they say, 'We believe,' and will not be tested with affliction?" (Qur'an 29:2)

A *hadith* from *Sahih Bukhari*, narrated by Abu Huraira (RA) quotes Prophet Muhammad (PBUH) as saying, "If Allah wants to do good to somebody, He afflicts him with trials." Another hadith tells us, "Do not worry [about the pains of a disease], it will be expiation for your sins." (Bukhari, vol. 7, hadith #548, page 373).

Sickness and disease test the human spirit, as in the case of Ayyub (AS) and Yaqub (AS), the prophets Job and Jacob respectively. *Sabr* and *shukr* (patience and gratitude) are vital keys in the healing process.

See *Sabr* under AIDS TO HEALING.

A wise person would rather take on all the hardships in this world in order to enjoy eternal life in the Hereafter. Always recite, *"Rabbana aateena fidduniya hasana wa fil aakhirati hasana wa qina azabannar"* — "Our Lord! Give us in this world that which is good and in the Hereafter that which is good, and save us from the torment of the Fire!" (Qur'an 2:201)

216. **I know that I cannot expect the comforts of home in the hospital anyway, but can I bring my own favourite pillow to the hospital?**

A: Yes, certainly. Remember to take it back again and be very careful that you don't carry any infections home.

217. I want to keep my medical problem to myself, from my nosy friends, especially regarding my hospitalization. What is the best way?

A: One way to keep your neighbours and friends away from this news is by telling them that you are going away for some time and you will contact them only after coming back.

218. What's the Islamic perspective on CPR (cardio-pulmonary resuscitation)?

A: Ulema as well as scientists do not give a definite answer on this subject, although CPR is performed under a variety of conditions. In my view, CPR is a medical approach to sustain life. It must be practiced. After all, Rasool Allah (PBUH) has directed us to make use of medical treatment. (See Abu Dawud, vol 3, hadith #3846). A scientific paper by Khalid L. Rehman, M.D., of Staten Island, NY, published in the *Journal of the Islamic Medical Association* (Vol. 25, 1993, page 20), sheds some light on the subject. Discretion of the individual or his living will, then his family is the answer. (Refer Qur'an 3:145, 10:56, 17:33, 39:42)

219. What is cupping? I've read in some *hadith* that Prophet Muhammad (PBUH) recommends cupping under certain medical conditions?

A: Prophet Muhammad (PBUH) recommended cupping for some medical problems. This involves inverting a cup with a flame in it over that part of the body where treatment is needed. When the burning material extinguishes, the vacuum created in the cup sucks the muscles, causing blood to rush to the area, which is incised, for bleeding. Today, *Allah Ta'ala* has given us far more sophisticated treatments. (Ref. Bukhari, vol 7, hadith #584)

220. **Can I use my cellular phone during my stay in hospital so I don't have to pay rental fee for the hospital phone?**

A: Cellular phones can interfere with monitoring equipment in the hospital. Please do not use them inside the hospital premises.

221. **What is nosocomial disease?**

A: Occasionally, some problems originate during the stay in hospital even though hospital is supposed to be the safest place for the patient. Viral, bacterial or fungal infection is possible due to obvious negligence of sanitary and hygienic practices within hospital. Secondary diseases caused by such factors are termed nosocomial diseases.

222. **What is iatrogenic disease?**

A: Iatrogenic disease is a medical term to describe a disease contracted during medical procedures due to one's over sensitivity or as a side effect of a drug or even a technical error.

223. **I am scheduled for admission in the hospital next week. I am scared of any mishap!**

A: I'm sure you're not kidding. Mishaps can happen on the road, flight or anywhere, including hospitals. However, you don't have to worry about it if you trust in Allah (SWT).

224. **It is funny that there are two patients in my ward with the same family name!**

A: This kind of coincidence can lead to a possibility of a mix-up of medications or treatment, if the hospital file number or the bar code is overshadowed by the family name. It is quite smart to write your first (given) name in large bold letters and leave it near your bed.

Jokingly and diplomatically, remind the medical staff about this. Precaution doesn't hurt.

225. **For the first time, I entered the emergency room of the hospital for a minor cut. While the doctor was examining me, my heart started beating fast. I never had this experience before. Do you think I should have told this to the doctor?**

A: Do not withhold anything unusual about your health from your doctor. This situation of faster heartbeat is sometimes described as "white coat syndrome." You were simply scared to see the doctor in his white coat. Just relax. It's nothing to worry about. Just mention this to the doctor next time, so that he (or she) will take care of you tactfully while checking your blood pressure.

226. **Thanks to Allah (SWT) that my surgery was successful, disease is cured and I am relieved of my pains. How can I thank our Creator more?**

A: Perform *nafl salaat* to give thanks to Allah (SWT). Give charity, and say, *"Haada min fadli Rabbi Liyablowani-A'ashkuro-Am Akfor"* – "This is by the grace of my Lord to test me, whether I'm grateful or ungrateful." (Qur'an 27:40; see also 7:43, 28:70 and 45:36-37)

Alternatively, you may say, *"Alhamdu lillah allazi bena`amatehe tateem alsalahat"* – "All praises are for Allah by Whose favour good works are accomplished."

227. **I am going abroad next month. Do you have any suggestions regarding health care?**

A: If you have to take some medicines with you for use while you will be away, it is not the best idea to put them away in your luggage separately. Take the most important ones or a few doses of them with you in your carry-all bag. This is because the luggage could get lost, damaged or arrive late.

Keep up the good habit of washing your hands and simple hygiene wherever you go. It is better to eat less but healthy food. Peel your own fruits and eat. Consider health insurance. Talk to your doctor or visit the "Travel Clinic" if available.

228. I am sick of my disease. Hope there are no other kinds of diseases in this world.

A: I am afraid yes. There are moral diseases identified as "diseases of the heart" mentioned in Qur'an along with the cure. "It [the Qur'an] is a guide and a healing to those who believe." (Qur'an 2:10, 10:57, 13:27-28 and 41:44).

229. My disease is killing me fast and I am beginning to think my end has approached.

A: One will not be afraid of death once we understand the Creator, the Most Merciful and Beneficent. On the other hand, we love Him, and look forward to meet Him. If one loves the Most Beneficent God, *Ar-Rahman*, the problem of death will not arise.

230. I am shocked to learn that, sometimes, a healthy young person can develop a life-threatening illness all of a sudden.

A: Denial of certain symptoms is the problem among young people, especially males. Young and healthy people tend to ignore or postpone seeing a doctor in time. Common symptoms are chest pain, pain in the left arm and shoulder area, giddiness, disorientation, sudden loss of physical strength in arm or leg, etc. Do not sit around and wait for a disaster. See a doctor.

231. We are in our eighties. Our son and his family have been taking good care of us. Suddenly our son suffered a stroke and is hospitalized. We are devastated. We pray to Allah to take from our life to save his and to heal him.

A: You are undermining the generosity and mercy of *Allah Ta'ala* by bargaining with your life. *Allah Ta'ala* can favour your beloved son much more than you can wish. A parent's du'a, especially a mother's du'a, is a priceless treasure, here and in the hereafter, in the sight of Allah. Prayer is our strongest instrument of faith, so use it well. Ask for the good of all as in *Rabbana aatina fidduniya hasanatan wa fil aakhirati hasanatan wa qina azabannar.*

Wallahu A'lam

AIDS TO HEALING

1. *Sabr* (Patience)

Sickness is a time to practise patience, which often leads to a cure. *Sabr* is Arabic for endurance, forbearance, courage, fortitude, inner strength, calmness, perseverance and ability to support hardship. *Allah Subhanahu wa Ta'ala* likes people who demonstrate *sabr* in every calamity, and who trust in Allah, His Qur'an and His Messenger Muhammad (PBUH), and who practise piety.

"... and give glad tidings to the patient ones, who, when afflicted with calamity, say, 'Truly, to Allah we belong and to Him we shall return.' They're blessed and will be forgiven, and they'll receive His Mercy as they're the guided ones." (Qur'an 2: 155-157)

Says Allah (SWT): "Those who patiently persevere will truly receive a reward without measure!"

A person afflicted with a disease becomes very vulnerable. There's a tendency to lose faith in times of pain and sorrow. People then turn to anything or anyone who can help to reduce their distress. A Muslim demonstrates strong faith in Allah to cure sickness or disease and to replace sorrow with happiness.

Sabr is a *ni'ma* and sickness is a test from Allah (SWT). He tests only those whom He loves the most. All the prophets, e.g., Nooh, Ibrahim, Yaqub, Yusuf, Yunus, Musa, Isa (Nova, Abraham, Jacob, Joseph, Jonah, Moses, Jesus), and Muhammad, peace be upon them all, have gone through severe tests and shown their qualities of *sabr*. (Qur'an 46:35)

Allah (SWT) tests us in different ways — through a blessing or a calamity, disease or health, wealth or poverty, beauty or ugliness, and so on — and we the servants of Allah should show patience to pass these tests. In

Hadith Qudsi we read, "Allah's mercy prevails over His wrath." (Ref: Muslim, Bukhari, Nasai and Ibn Maja)

Our earthly existence is a transitory phase. However, we achieve eternal bliss in the Hereafter only by following Allah's commands and practising *sabr* coupled with thanks and gratitude, and by remembering Allah at all times.

You practise *sabr* by:

- Not complaining or cursing your fate
- Engaging in *zikr*
- Asking Allah (SWT) to keep us steadfast in *imaan*
- Gaining *taqwa* by giving charity
- Seeking *astaghfar* (Allah's forgiveness)
- Helping others who are in more difficulty than ourselves
- Reciting, listening or contemplating on the Qur'an
- Reading, finding out and trying to follow the examples of *sabr* practiced by the prophets, the Companions of Prophet Muhammad (PBUH) and the favoured servants of Allah, and --
- Always being thankful to Allah (SWT) for the good things He has bestowed on you.

One can think of more ways of thanking Allah (SWT) depending on one's own situation. For example, a person who has broken his leg and has a cast on it should be thankful that he has another leg to walk with, and the rest of his body is intact.

Even if your disease is life-threatening, and if every caregiver is helpless, be thankful to *Allah Subhanahu wa Ta'ala* and say *Alhamdulillah* that you can enjoy the *rizq* (bounty) of breathing, drinking water, thinking, talking, listening, seeing, etc.

You must be happy since your mind is still working right. You are blessed with *imaan* more than anything else! Perhaps you got a last-minute reprieve to ask pardon from your folks or colleagues whom you might have hurt in whatever way.

Abdullah (RA) narrates, "I visited the Prophet (PBUH) during his ailments and he was suffering from a high fever. I said, 'you have a high fever. Is it because you will have a double reward for it?' He said, 'yes, for no Muslim is afflicted with any harm, but that Allah (SWT) will remove his sins as the leaves of a tree fall down.'" (Bukhari, vol 7, hadith #565, page 383)

Sickness brings one closer to Allah and awakens us from our heedlessness. People, who have received the gift of cure from Allah after a prolonged and severe sickness, and those who've recovered from near-fatal accidents, have invariably changed their lives for the better. Sometimes Allah gives a physical disease as opposed to mental, to remedy our arrogance and egoism, which are the diseases of the soul.

Sickness is the law enforcer, which drags the person out of *ghaflath* and brings him to reality. Hence, in a way, a true Muslim is not afraid of any calamity which may befall him, but will practice *sabr, shukr* and, in turn, gain Allah's mercy and pleasure.

A patient who is confined to his hospital bed, away from the hustle and bustle of the outside world and the responsibilities of life, can best use his/her time to learn the purpose of life in this world and prepare for the Day of Judgment. He or she must change his or her attitude that the hospital bed is a prison, and instead choose to see it as an open school and masjid, where one can learn and practice *sabr, shukr, zikr* (remembrance of Allah), *tawakkul, taqwa* and *imaan*.

At the time of sickness, one should be highly thankful to Allah (SWT) because everyone who sees or knows that you are sick, asks *du'a* and wishes for an early and complete recovery. Often, the *saleheen* (the pious ones) make *du'a* for the people in distress. This is itself a blessing for the sick.

Finally, the best thing is to show mercy on youngsters, respect to elders, love to all, and forgiveness to all those who have come into your life at one time or another, including your caregivers and hospital staff. In your *du'a*, remember those who might have brought annoyance to you and forgive them. By forgiving others, you may not lose much, but you will certainly win the *maghfirah* (pardon) from Allah (SWT).

By this, I do not mean that you are encouraging these parties to go ahead and bother you, but simply that you do not worry about their actions and let Allah take care of these things. By forgiving, you will see that, psychologically, you feel a lot lighter, freer and healthier. This is in addition to the best reward from Allah.

In fact, a sick person has to practice *sabr* to the extent that you say *Shukr Alhamdulillah* (Thanks, praise be to God) no matter what. In this regard, Prophet Muhammad (PBUH) says, "Do not curse fever. It expiates sins as furnace removes rust of iron." (Muslim Vol. 4, H 6244)

Our *du'a* therefore is: *Ya Allah*, kindly do not put us under Your test for which we are not fit and we are certainly weak and impatient. If we fail in Your test, we could be sinners. Forgive us. After all we are Your creations and You are our Lord and we do have to return to You. *Aameen*.

Other Qur'anic references concerning *sabr* are: 2:45, 152-157, 214, 3:102-104, 186, 200, 8:46, 8:66, 10:62-65, 109, 21:83, 26:78-87, 31:17, 39:10 and Sura 93.

There is no shortage of *ahadith* on this subject either!

2. Relevant verses

"We (Allah) will surely try you with danger, hunger, and loss of wealth and lives and fruits (crop), but give glad tidings to the patient (Sabir) – those who, when afflicted with a calamity, say, 'Indeed we belong to Allah, and indeed to Him we will return.' Those are the ones upon whom are bestowed (Salawaat) and mercy from their Lord and those are the ones who are (indeed) guided." (Qur'an 2:155-157)

෪ ○ ෨

"Our Lord! Give us good in this world and good in the Hereafter, and defend us from the torment of the Fire!" (Qur'an 2:201)

෪ ○ ෨

"O you who believe! Fear Allah (practice piety by obeying all His commandments), as He should be feared (with love, gratefulness and remembrance), and die not except in full submission to Allah." (Qur'an 3:102)

෪ ○ ෨

"... Say: 'Allah suffices me: there is no god but He: on Him is my trust. He is the Lord of the Throne (of Glory) Supreme!'" (Qur'an 9:129)

෪ ○ ෨

"Behold! Verily on the friends of Allah there is no fear, nor shall they grieve. Those who believe and (constantly) guard against evil, for them are Glad Tidings, in the life of the Present and in the Hereafter: no change can there be in the Words of Allah. This is indeed the supreme success." (Qur'an 10:64 [63-65])

ᢙ 〇 ᠍

"Those who believe and whose hearts find satisfaction in the remembrance of Allah: for without doubt, in the remembrance of Allah, do hearts find satisfaction (comfort)." (Qur'an 13:28)

ᢙ 〇 ᠍

"There issues from within their bellies a drink (honey) of varying colors, wherein is healing for mankind: verily in this is a Sign for those who give thought." (Qur'an 16:69)

ᢙ 〇 ᠍

"And We (Allah) send down in the Qur'an that which is a healing and a mercy to those who believe: to the unjust, it causes nothing but loss after loss." (Qur'an 17:82)

ᢙ 〇 ᠍

"… Verily, distress has seized me, and You are the Most Merciful of all those who show mercy." (Qur'an 21:83)

ᢙ 〇 ᠍

"… And O you believers! Turn you all together towards Allah, that you may attain Bliss." (Qur'an 24:31)

ଔ ◯ ଚ

"(Allah, Lord and Cherisher of the worlds) Who created me, and it is He Who guides me; Who gives me food and drink, and when I am sick, it is He Who cures me; Who will cause me to die; and then to live (again); and Who, I hope, will forgive me my faults on the Day of Judgment; O my Lord! Bestow on me, and join me with the righteous; Grant me a truthful (perfect) report in the later generation; Make me one of the inheritors of the garden of bliss." (Qur'an 26:78-85)

ଔ ◯ ଚ

"And put your trust in Allah, for Allah is sufficient as Trustee." (Qur`an 33:3)

ଔ ◯ ଚ

"No kind of calamity can occur except by the permission of Allah; and if anyone believes in Allah, (Allah) guides his heart right; for Allah knows all things." (Qur'an 64:11)

ଔ ◯ ଚ

3. Relevant *Ahadith*

"Make use of medical treatment, for Allah (SWT) has not made a disease without appointing a remedy for it, with the exception of one disease, namely old age." (Abu Dawud, vol 3, hadith 3846)

❧　○　❦

"There are two blessings, which many people lose: Health and free time for doing good." (Bukhari, vol 8, hadith 421)

❧　○　❦

"I seek refuge in Almighty Allah (SWT) and in His Power from that which I feel and fear." (Muslim)

❧　○　❦

"No calamity befalls a Muslim but that Allah expiates some of his sins because of it, even though it were the prick he receives from a thorn." (Bukhari, vol 7, hadith 544)

❧　○　❦

"Feed the hungry, visit the sick, and have the captives set free." (Bukhari, vol 7, hadith 552)

❧　○　❦

"Whenever the Prophet went to a patient, he used to say to him, "Don't worry, it will be expiation (for your sins)," a Bedouin said, "You say expiation? No, it is but a fever that is boiling or harassing an old man and will lead him to his grave without his will." The Prophet said, "Then yes, it is so." (Bukhari, vol 7, hadith 560)

ଔ   ◯   ଔ

"No disease Allah (SWT) created but that He created its treatment." (Bukhari, vol 7, hadith 582)

ଔ   ◯   ଔ

"If you hear of an outbreak of plague in a land, do not enter it; but if the plague breaks out in a place while you are in it, do not leave that place." (Bukhari, vol 7, hadith # 624)

ଔ   ◯   ଔ

"During his fatal illness, The Prophet (PBUH) used to recite the *Mu'auwidhat (Surah An-Naas & Surah Al-Falaq)* and then blow his breath over his body..." (Bukhari, vol 7, hadith 631)

ଔ   ◯   ଔ

"Whenever a person gets sick (who has difficulty in performing *ibada* physically), his deeds are recorded for him in accordance with what he used to do when he was well." (Bukhari, in al-Adab ul-Mufrad, # 501)

ଔ   ◯   ଔ

"None of you should die without having good expectations in Allah (SWT)." (Muslim)

ଔ   ◯   ଔ

Ibn Abbas (RA): "Healing is in three things: cupping, a gulp of honey or cauterizing. But I forbid my followers to use cauterization." (Bukhari, vol 7, hadith 584)

CS ○ SO

Abu Huraira (RA) reported that the Prophet (PBUH) said that Allah (SWT) says: "I am with My servant when he remembers Me and his lips move to mention Me." (Ahmed and Ibn Majah)

CS ○ SO

Allah (SWT) says, "When I take (away) my servant's sight, and he remains patient and seeks My reward for it, I approve of no reward for him less than Paradise." (At-Tirmithi)

CS ○ SO

"The magnitude of the reward is in accordance with the magnitude of the affliction. When Allah (SWT) loves some people, He afflicts them." (At-Tirmithi)

CS ○ SO

Abu Huraira (RA) states that the Prophet said: "When Allah created the creatures He wrote in the Book which is with Him in the highest heaven: 'My mercy shall prevail over My anger.' Another version says: 'My mercy covers My anger', and yet another version says: 'My compassion surpasses My anger.'" (Bukhari & Muslim)

CS ○ SO

Abu Huraira (RA) reported " I heard Allah's Messenger saying, "There is healing in blackseed for all diseases except death." (Blackseed is known by different names in different regions: *Nigella sativa;* Habbat-ul Barakaat; Kalonji.) (Bukhari, vol 7, hadith 592)

ロ ○ ロ

Mu'adh b. Jabal reported that the Prophet (PBUH) said, "If anyone's last words are 'There is no god but Allah', he will enter Paradise." (Abu Dawud)

ロ ○ ロ

Narrated Abu Huraira (RA), Allah's Apostle (PBUH) said, "Allah says, 'I have nothing to give but Paradise as a reward to My believer slave, who, if I cause his dear friend (or relative) to die, will be patient (and hope for Allah's reward).'" (Bukhari)

ロ ○ ロ

Narrated Abdullah (RA): 'The Prophet (PBUH) said, "... No Muslim is afflicted with any harm but that his sins will be annulled as the leaves of a tree fall down." (Bukhari, vol 7, hadith 565)

ロ ○ ロ

The Prophet (PBUH) used to say: *"Alhamdu lillah allazi bena'amatehe tateem alsalahat."* ("All praises are for Allah by Whose favour good works are accomplished," for a good news.) Otherwise, *"Alhamdu lillah Ala kol haal."* ("All praises are for Allah under all circumstances.")

ロ ○ ロ

See also the *du'a* in answer to Question 115.

4. Relevant *du'as* of Prophet Muhammad
(PBUH)

اَللّٰهُمَّ رَبَّ النَّاسِ اَذْهِبِ الْبَأْسَ اِشْفِهِ اَنْتَ الشَّافِي

لَا شِفَاءَ إِلاَّ شِفَاؤُكَ شِفَاءًلَا يُغَادِرُ سَقَماً

"Allahumma rabb an-nas, athhib il-ba's, washfi ant ash-shafi, la shifa illa shifauk, la yughadiru saqama." (O Allah, Lord of the people, take away the hardship, and give cure – You are the One Who cures, and there is no cure except from You – a cure that will not leave any sickness behind.) (Bukhari, vol 7, hadith 579, and Muslim).

اَسْأَلْ اللّٰهَ الْعَظِيمَ، رَبَّ الْعَرْشِ الْعَظِيم أَنْ يَشْفِيكَ

"As'al ul-Lah al-azim, rabb al-arsh il-azim an yashfiyak" (I ask Allah the Great, the Lord of the great Throne, to cure.) Make this *du'a* seven times. (Abu Dawood and At-Tirmithi)

لَابَأَسَ، طَهُورٌ إِنْ شَاءَ اللّٰه

"La ba's, tahurun in sha'Allah" (No harm [may befall you]; may this [sickness] be a purifier [for your sins] – with Allah's will.) (Bukhari)

اَللّٰهُمَّ اَشْفِ عَبْدَكَ يَنْكِّى لَكَ عَدُواً، اَوْيَمْشِي لَكَ إِلى صَلاةٍ

"Allahummm ashfi `abdak, yanka laka aduwan aw yamshi laka ila salaat" (O Allah, cure your servant, he would then upset an enemy of Yours, or walk to a prayer in obedience to You.) (Abu Dawud)

اَللّٰهُمَّ أَحْيِنِى مَادَامَتِ الْحَيَاةُ خَيْرًالِّى وَتَوَفَّنِى إِذَا كَانَتِ الْوَفَاةُ خَيْرًالِّي

وَاجْعَلِ الْحَيَاةَ زِيَادَةً لِّي فِي كُلِّ خَيْرٍ، وَاجْعَلِ الْمَوْتَ رَاحَةً لِّيْ مِنْ كُلِّ شَرٍّ

"Allahumma ahint ma damat il-hayatu khayran li wa tawaffani itha kaanat il-wafatu kharan li. Waj al il-hayata ziyadatan li fi kulli khayr, waj'al il-mawta raahatan li min kulli sharr" (O Allah let me live as long as life is better for me; let me die when death is better for me; let life be a means for me to increase in all that is good; and let death be a rest for me from all evil.) (Bukhari)

اَللّٰهُمَّ اِنِّى أَسْأَلُكَ فِعْلَ الْخَيْرَاتِ، وَتَرْكَ الْمُنْكَرَاتِ، وَحُبَّ الْمَسَاكِينِ

وَأَنْ تَغْفِرَلِيْ وَتَرْحَمَنِي ، وَإِذَاأَرَدْتَ فِتْنَةً فِيْ قَوْمٍ فَتَوَفَّنِي غَيْرَ مَفْتُونٍ

Allahumma inni as`aluka fil al-khayraat, wa-tarak al-munkaraat, wa-hubb al-masaakin, wa `an taghfira li wa-tarhamni. Wa itha aratta fitnatan fi qawmin fatawaffani ghayra maftoon" (O Allah! Enable me to do good deeds, avoid evil deeds, and love the poor; and forgive me and have mercy upon me. And if You will to send chaos over the people, take my life without being puzzled (in my *Deen*.) (Ahmed, at-Tirmithi)

اَللّٰهُمَّ إِنِّي أَسْأَلُكَ تَاجِلْ لِعَافِيَتِكَ ، وَصَبْراً عَلَى بَلِيَّاتِكَ

وَخُرُوجًا مِنَ الدُّنْيَا إِلَى رَحْمَتِكَ

"Allahumma inni as'aluka ta`jila aafiyatika, wa-sabran 'ala baliyyatika, wa-khuroojan min ad-dunya ila rahmatik" (O Allah, I ask You to quicken Your cure, give me patience with Your affliction, and let my departure from this world be Your mercy.) (al-Haakim, ad-Daylami)

اَعُوذُ بِعِزَّةِ اللهِ وَقُدْرَتِهِ مِنْ شَرِّمَا اَجِدُوَاُحَاذِرُ

"Aauzu bi izzati Ilahi wa qudratihi min sharri ma ajidu wa uhaazir"
(I seek refuge in Allah's eminence and power from all that I feel and fear
— place your hand on the area of pain, utter it seven times after reciting
Bismillah three times.) (Muslim)

اَللّهُمَّ غَارَتِ النُّجُومْ وَ هَدَأَتِ الْعُيُونُ وَ أَنْتَ حَيِّي قَيُّومْ

لَا تَأْخُذُكَ سِنَةٌ وَلَا نَوْمْ يَا حَيِّي يَا قَيُّومْ اَللّهُمَّ اَهْدِئْ لَيْلِيْ وَأَنِمْ عَيْنِيْ

*"Allahumma ghaarat aln-nujum, wa hada'at al-uyun wa anta
hayyun qayyoom, laa ta'khudhuka sinatun wa laa nawm; Allahumma
ihdi laylee wa anim 'aynee."* (O Allah, stars have set, (my) eyes have
rested. You are the Ever-Alive, the Self-Subsisting source of all being; neither slumber nor sleep overtakes You. O The Living, The Subsisting. O
Allah! Make my night comforting to me, and bring sleep unto my eyes.)
Reported by Ibn al-Sunni on the authority of Zayd b. Thabit, who was
taught this *du'a* by *Rasool Allah* (PBUH) for insomnia.

الْحَمْدُ لِلهِ الَّذِي بِنِعْمَتِهِ تَتِمُّ الصَّالِحَاتُ

"Alhamdu lillah allazi bena'amatehe tateem alsaalihaat" (All praises
are for Allah (SWT) by Whose favour good works are accomplished.) (Ibn as-
Sunni)

Reported by al-Tabrani and Ibn Shaybah on the authority of Khalid b. al-Walid that he said: "I was suffering from insomnia and when I reported it to the Prophet (PBUH), he asked me, 'Shall I teach you certain words which if you were to recite you would sleep better?' then he said: Say:

اَللّٰهُمَّ رَبِّ السَّمٰوَاتِ السَّبْعِ وَمَا أَظَلَّتْ، وَرَبَّ الْأَرَاضِينِ وَمَا أَقَلَّتْ وَرَبَّ الشَّيَاطِينِ اَمَا أَظَلَّتْ كُنْ لِي جَاراً مِنْ شَرِّ خَلْقِكَ اَجْمَعِينْ أَنْ يَفْرُطَ عَلَىَّ أَحَدٌ مِنْهُمْ أَوأَن يَطْفَىٰ، عَزَّ جَارُكَ وَتَبَارَكِ إِسْمُكَ

Allaahumma rabba al-samaawaati alssab'wa maa azalaat wa rabba al-aradheena wa maa aqallat, wa rabba al-sheshayaateeni wa maa adhallat, kun lee jaaran min sharri khalqika ajma'eena an yafruta 'alayya ahadun minhum aw an yatghaa, 'azza jaaruka, wa tabaaraka ismuka. (O Allah, O You Who are the Lord of the seven heavens and whatever they shelter, and the earths and whatever they contain, and You Who are the Lord of devils and whomsoever they mislead, You be my Gaurdian-Protector against the evils of all of Your creatures; guard me against their intrusions. Noble is the one who enjoys Your Protection and Glorified is Your name.)

The reporter comments: "Accordingly, Khalid said these words, and then he slept well."

رَبَّنَآ اٰتِنَا فِيى الدُّنْيَا حَسَنَةً وَفِي الْآخِرَةِ حَسَنَةً وَقِنَا عَذَابَ النَّارِ

"Rabbana aatina fidduniya hasanatan wa fil aakhirati hasanatan wa qina azabannar." (Our Lord! Give us good in this world and good in the Hereafter and defend us from the torment of [Hell] fire.) (Qur'an 2:201)

اَللّٰهُمَّ اِنِّى مَسَّنِيَ الـضُّرُّ وَاَنْتَ اَرْحَمُ الرَّاحِمِينْ

"Inni massani-adduru wa anta arhamar-rahimeen." (Lo! Adversity has seized me, but You are the Most Merciful.) (Qur'an 21:83)

لَا إِلٰهَ إِلَّا اَنْتَ سُبْحَانَكَ اِنِّى كُنْتُ مِنَ الضَّالِمِينْ

"Laa ilaha illa anta subhanaka inni kuntu minaz-zalimeen." (There is no god but You, glory to You; I was indeed of the wrong doers.) (Qur'an 21:87)

5. Humour for patients and caregivers

Humour, amusement and a little laughter of course is a great medicine. Prophet Muhammad (PBUH) liked jokes. He once jokingly told an old lady, "Look, your nose is in-between your eyes." On another occasion, he told an old lady that old ladies do not go to Jannah. The lady was sad, soon the Prophet said, all the ladies in Jannah will enjoy youth and they will not be old there."

∞ ○ ∞

The doctor told the patient before colonoscopy, "You do not have to smile during this filming procedure!"

∞ ○ ∞

Home is the place where you can scratch wherever you want to. In the hospital?

∞ ○ ∞

A newly wed bride of a doctor received the first letter from her husband who was on a tour. She could not read his handwriting till the pharmacist helped her.

∞ ○ ∞

The patient was asked why he started using cigarette holder while smoking. He said, the doctor had asked him to keep away from cigarette.

∞ ○ ∞

If you run a graph of cost of hospitalization and progress in medical sciences, they run parallel and steep high.

ଔ ◯ ଛ

We are living in a scientific age where there is often a need to take a second opinion from another doctor.

ଔ ◯ ଛ

I wish the researchers stop working on miracles of medical treatment and start working on affordable treatment methods.

ଔ ◯ ଛ

I guess hospitals must be saving a lot in their budget by shortening the length of examination gowns of the patients.

ଔ ◯ ଛ

An outpatient to the doctor: Your staff is very efficient. The nurse always arranges two patients in two rooms at the same time, ready for your examination.

Doctor: Yes, my staff and I like to kill two (birds) in one shot!

ଔ ◯ ଛ

Some people live on borrowed money, yet some patients on borrowed time.

ଓ ◯ ଇ

One outpatient: It is so nice to take a hot bath before retiring.

Another: I have seven more years to retire!

ଓ ◯ ଇ

Learn to love the uphill, rest becomes nothing but downhill.

ଓ ◯ ଇ

Patient: O God, please give me patience, but hurry, hurry please.

ଓ ◯ ଇ

Patient to the doctor: I had a hard time going to washroom during my visit to Turkey.

Doctor: Were you not eating and sleeping regularly?

Patient: Everything was okay, but the entrance to the washrooms cost 500 Turkish lira!

ଓ ◯ ଇ

Patient: I have a problem with my right nostril?

Doctor: I will give you a referral to another specialist because my specialty is in the left nostril!

A Medical Lexicon (Between You & Me)

Antibody – *against everybody*
Artery – *the study of fine paintings*
Bacteria – *back door to a cafeteria*
Benign – *what you be after your eighth birthday*
Bowel – *letter like a, e, i, o, u*
Caesarian section – *a district in Rome*
Cardiology – *advanced study of poker playing*
CAT scan – *searching for a lost pet*
Coma – *punctuation mark*
Cortisone – *area around local courthouse*
Cyst – *short for sister*
Diagnosis – *person with a slanted nose*
Dislocation – *in this place*
Duodenum – *couple in jeans*
Enema – *not a friend*
False labour – *pretending to work while on unemployment benefits*
Feces – *nasty countenance*
Gallbladder – *bladder of a girl*
Genes – *blue denim*
Groin – *to mash to pulp; also, to smile*
Hernia – *she is close by*
Hymen – *simultaneous greeting to several males*
Impotent – *distinguished, well-known*
Labour pain – *hurt at work, hence on compensation*
Lactose – *person without toes*
Liposuction – *a French kiss*
Lymph – *walk unsteadily*
Menopause – *slang for "I no wait"*
Microbes – *small dressing gowns*
Obesity – *city of Obe, somewhere*
Pacemaker – *winner of Nobel Peace Prize*
Pleural fluid – *a cocktail of liquids*

Protein – *fond of teen porn*
Pulse – *grain, such as daal, a pulse*
Pus – *small cat*
Red blood cell count – *Dracula*
Rupture – *ecstasy*
Secretion – *hiding something!*
Semen – *sailors*
Serum – *sailor's drink, from Treasure Island*
Subcutaneous – *not cute enough*
Suture – *"what do you want?"*
Tablet – *small table*
Testes – *senses experienced by tongue*
Tumor – *extra pair*
Ultrasound – *radical noise, as in a fish market*
Urine – *opposite of "You're out"*
Varicose – *warmly clad, as in thermal underwear*
Vas deferens – *extremely different*
Vein – *"at what time?"*
Vitreous humour – *both witty and funny*

A selective bibliography

1.   A Rights Advice Guide, published by The Ontario Advocacy Commission. ON Canada.

2.   Abdalati, Hammudah. "Islam in Focus" American Trust Publication, 10900 W. Washington Street Indianapolis, IN 46231, USA   ISBN   0-89259-000-9

3.   Ali, A Yusuf. "The Holy Quran, Translation and commentary" Hafner Publishing Company,   New York, USA.   There have been several publications from different companies. One published in 1411 Hijra (1979 CE) from The Ministry of Hajj and Endowments, The Kingdom of Saudi Arabia P.O. Box 3561 Al-Madinah Al-Munawarah is the revised edition.

4.   Al-Jibaly, Muhammad. "Inevitable Journey". Part I: Sickness: Regulations & Exhortations.
     Al-Kitaab & as-Sunnah Publishing
     P.O.Box 2542 Arlington, Texas 76004.

5.   Al-Qaradawi, Yusuf. "The lawful and the Prohibited in Islam" International Islamic Federation of Student Organizations P.O Box 8631 Salimiah – Kuwait 22057.

6.   Ashraf, Sh. Muhammad. "Sunan Abu Dawud" English translation with explanatory notes by Prof. Ahmad Hasan, in three volumes. Published by Publishers & Booksellers, 7-Aibak road (New Anarkali) Lahore, Pakistan. Reprint 1993

7.   Athar, Shahid MD. "Health Guidelines from Qur`an & Sunnah" Islamic Horizons, Apl.1986

8.   Badawi, Dr. Jamal of Halifax, Canada.   Discussions available on audiotapes and publications.

9.   Consent to Treatment, A Guide to the Act. Published by the Consent to Treatment Health Information Centre. Ministry of Health, 80 Grosvenor St., 8th floor, Toronto ON, M7A 1S2.

10.   Ebrahim, Abul Fadl Mohsin. "Abortion, Birth Control & Surrogate Parenting, An Islamic perspective" American Trust Publications. ISBN-0-89259-081-5.

11.   El Hashmi, Elsheikh Syed Mubarik Ali Jilani Qadri. "Quranic Psychiatry".
        Published by Zavia Books, International Open University, New York, USA
        Islamabad Pakistan.

12.   Elkadi, Ahmed. "Health & Healing in the Qur`an", published in Islamic
        Perspectives in Medicine, Editor, Athar S, American Trust Publications,
        Indianapolis, 1993, PP 117-122.

13.   Hathout, Hassan. "Reading the Muslim Mind". American Trust Publications
        2622 East Main Street Plainfield, Indiana 46168-2703. Printed 1997.

14.   Health Care Consent, and several other related publications; Health
        Information Centre, Ministry of Health, 80 Grosvenor Street, 8th Floor, Toronto
        M7A 1S2.Tel. 416-327-7730, Toll-Free: 1-800-461-2036.

15.   Idrees, Moulana Muhammad. "Hasan Haseen", An Urdu language book.
        Published by Taj Co. Ltd., Karachi, Pakistan.

16.   Islahi, Muhammad Yusuf. "Everyday Fiqh" Vol.1 English version by Abdul
        Aziz Kamal. Islamic Publication Ltd. 13-E Shahalam Market Lahore Pakistan.

17.   Karim, Al-Haj Maulana Fazlul. "Al-Hadis" Published in 4 volumes by The
        Book House. Trust Building, Urdu Bazaar, Lahore, Pakistan.

18.   Khan, Dr. Muhammad Muhsin. "Sahih Al-Bukhari" Ahadith in Arabic—
        English in 9 volumes. Translation Islamic University, Al-Medina Al-Munauwara.
        Published by Dar Al Arabia, PO Box 6089 Beirut Lebanon.

19.   Maclean's, Canada's Weekly Newsmagazine, Jan. 10, 2000 – "Looking into
        The Future Medicine in 2020"

20.   Moudoodi, Abul A'ala. "Fundamentals of Islam" published by Idara
        Tarjuman-ul-Quran, Idhara, Lahore, Pakistan.

21.   Maudoodi, Abul A'la. "The Meaning of Qur'an", English translation of
        Tafheemul Qur'an (Urdu), Published by The Board of Islamic Publications,
        Delhi 110006, India.

22.   Maudoodi, Abul A'la Tafhimul Qur'an (in Urdu), Published by Markazi
        Maktaba Islami, Delhi 6, India.

23. Pickthal, Muhammad Marmaduke. "The Glorious Qur'an" Text and Explanatory Translation. Library of Congress Card Number 77-71254.

24. Rahimuddin, Prof. Muhammad. "Muwatta, Imam Malik" Translation, Revised edition 1985. Taj company, 3151, Turkman Gate, Delhi-110006 India.

25. Siddiqi, Abdul Hamid. Translation rendered into English in 4 volumes. "Sahih Muslim" by Imam Muslim. Seventh edition, 1987. Published by Nusrat Ali Nasri for Kitab Bhavan, 1214, Kalan Mahal, Darya Ganj, New Delhi-110002 India.

26. Syed, Amjad. Co-author, "Multifaith Prayer / Meditation Book". Published by The Credit Valley Hospital, # 2200 Eglinton Ave. West, Mississauga ON L5M 2N1 Canada. 1998

27. Syed, Amjad. Co-author, "Religious and Spiritual Beliefs and Practices in Health Care", Chapter on Islamic practices. Published by the Pastoral Care Services, The Mississauga Hospital. Canada. 1996.

28. Syed, Dr. Ibrahim B. "Smoking is Unlawful in Islam." Journal of Islamic Medical Association, Vol. 15, # 4 Oct. 1983 pp. 110-112.

29. Syed, Jaffer. "Organ Donation Issues in the Muslim Community" University of Toronto Faculty of Medicine. April 25, 1996.

30. Vardit, Rispler-Chaim. "Islamic Medical Ethics in the Twentieth Century". Published by E. J. Brill, New York 1993

31. Zeno, Muhammad bin Jamil. "The pillars of Islam & Iman" Dar-us-Salam Publications, Riyadh, Saudi Arabia.

Interesting and useful references

1. Al Qarni, Ayed Bin Abdullah. "La Tahzan" (Don't Be Sad). Maktab Albalad Al Ameen, Jam-e-Al Azhar, Cairo. (Arabic book)

2. Attamimi, Asshaikh Abu Abdullah Abdul Ghani bin Ahmed. "Ma'al Mareed", an Arabic publication by Daarul Samee al Nashr Wattauzia, Riyad, Saudi rabia. This is exceptionally well written 40 pages booklet for the sick. Any believer, after reading this, will feel better InshaAllah. I pray and wish, this was translated into other languages too and made available to the sick. –Amjad Syed, Author.

3. Council of Jurists, Fourth session (Medical and Fiqh viewpoints). Jedda S.A. Feb.6-11,1988, regarding "Body Organs Donation". 1989 Contemporary Research Journal, P.O. Box 1918, Riyad S.A.

4. Fiqh an-Nawazil –"Shari'ah Rulings of new issues". Vol.1, pp 215-236 Article # 4 printed by Maktabah ar-Rushd, Riyad, 1407.

5. Fisher, R. "A guide to end-of-life care for seniors" University of Toronto and University of Ottawa (Spring 2000). ISBN: 0-9687122-0-7

6. Gatrad, A. R. Muslim "Customs Surrounding Death, Bereavement, Postmortem examinations, and Organ Transplants". British Medical Journal. 1994. 309 ; 521-3

7. Ghanem, Isam. "Islamic Medical Jurisprudence" London. 1982. 62-63.

8. Islamic Horizons (Jan-Feb 2002), Plainfield, IN, USA.

9. Journal of Islamic Medical Association of USA and Canada. PO Box # 38 Plainfield, IN 46168-9904 USA Islamic Ethical Issues.

10. Myss, Caroline Ph.D. "Anatomy of Spirit". (Medical Intuitive).

11. Myss, Caroline Ph.D. "Why People Cannot Heal and How They Can"

12. Nursing Times newsfeature: "Life Giving Fatwa". July 19, 1995. 91 (29): 14-15.

13. Rasheed, H. Z. A. Organ Donation and Transplantation: A Muslim Viewpoint. Transplantation Proceedings. 1992.24(5): 2116-2117.

14. Rispler-Chaim, Vardit. Islamic Medical Ethics in the Twentieth Century. E. J. Brill. New York. 1993. 28-44.

15. Sarwar, Ghulam. "Islam, Belief and Teaching" published by the Muslim Educational Trust, 130 Strout Green Road, London, N4 3R2, UK.

16. Sialkoti, M. Sadiq. "Morals and Manners in Islam" Translated by M. Rafiq Khan, Idaratul-Buhoosil Islamia, Jamia Salafia, Varanasi, India.

17. Syed, Amjad. Language Communication Guide for Hospital Patients and Visitors. This booklet, containing common phrases in 23 languages, was compiled in 1997 at Trillium Health Centre, Mississauga, for patients who could not speak English. This is in the hospital intranet system since 2000.

18. Videotapes on various subjects of Islam are available in many Islamic bookstores. For example: a) "Fight Pain with Patience & Prayer" by Br. Ezz E Gad of "Reflections on Islam T.V. program" Tape # 0412. Available from "Reflections on Islam" P.O. Box # 375, Station P, Toronto ON M5S 2S9 Canada; b) "Islamic Perspectives on Modern Medical Advances", a Forum arranged by I.S.S.R.A in Toronto Canada, in early 1990s. Here, we can wittness discussion, and Q/A by Muslim Ulema and Physicians.

Some Email Addresses and Websites

NB: This list is by no means conclusive. It is intended only as an introduction.

http://www.youngmuslims.ca/online_library/

www.al-islam.com You will find many relevant addresses through this.

isna@isnacanada.com Islamic Society of North America, HQ, # 2200 South Sheridan Way, Mississauga Ontario Canada L5J 2M4 Phone # 905-403-8406, Ext. 207, Fax # 905-403-8409

imana@aol.com, www.imana.org - Islamic Medical Association of North America, PO Box 38, Plainfield, IN 46168 USA. Tel: (630) 852-2122, Fax (630) 435-1429

http://astrolabe.muslimsonline.com/ - Islamic books, videos, software and audio

http://www.soundvision.com/life/zakatcalc.shtml

www.rehma.org - info@rehma.org - Muslim Elder Forum Rehma, Toronto ON, Canada.

www.cpca.net - National organizations can be spread under five main care categories: home care and home assistance; transportation; assistive services; palliative care and counseling; and support.

www.alzheimer.ca - Alzheimer's Association

www.arthritis.ca - Arthritis Society

www.diabetes.ca - Diabetes Association

For palliative care and assistive devices: www.vaxxine.com/pallcare

www.med.mcgill.ca/orgs/palcare/copchome.htm

www.thecareguide.com

www.utoronto.ca/seniors

A General Glossary

*Translating Arabic into English often calls for copious explanatory notes
in order to appreciate the original meanings of Islamic words and concepts.
The following glossary affords only a minimal explanation.*

Aaqira – Last Day (Day of Judgment).

Al Fateha – Opening chapter of the Qur'an.

Alhamdulillah – "All praises are to Allah," a common phrase on the lips of Muslims.

A'lim – A Muslim well schooled in Islam.

Allah – Proper name for God used by Muslims and Arabic-speaking Christians.

Allahu Akbar – "Allah is the Greatest."

Allah Ta'ala – Allah, the Most High.

Aqiqa – The first shaving of head of a Muslim baby.

Asr – Late afternoon *salaat,* one of the five daily obligatory prayers.

Ayat, ayaat – A verse from the Qur'an; *ayaat* is the plural.

Ayatul-Kursi – Verse 255 of Chapter 2 in the Qur'an, associated with bountiful *barakaat.*

Barakaat – Allah's blessings

Bismillah – In the name of Allah, a phrase on the lips of a Muslim before starting anything.

Darood – Part of the recitation during *salaat.*

Dhabiha – Meat of a permissible animal slaughtered according to Islamic code.

Da'wah – Invitation (to the faith).

Deen – The religion taught by Prophet Muhammad; a complete way of life.

Du'a – Invocation or supplication. Muslims pray to and petition only Allah (SWT).

Eid – A happy day; celebration of a festival, as in *Eid-ul-fitr,* or *Eid-ul-Adha.*

Fajr – Dawn prayer at first light; one of the five daily obligatory prayers.

Fard –Obligatory deeds ordained by Allah; *faraid* is plural.

Fatwa – A religious verdict given by a *mufti* on the basis of Qur'an and *Sunnah.*

Fidya – A charity that becomes compulsory when a Muslim is unable to carry on certain *fard.*

Fiqh –Islamic jurisprudence regarding law and its application.

Ghaflat – Heedlessness.

Ghaib – Knowledge known to Allah only.

Ghurur – Pride, arrogance, haughtiness.

Ghusl – Full bath according to Islamic code.

Hadith – The traditions, anything that Prophet Muhammad (PBUH) said or did or agreed upon; *ahadith* is the plural.

Hadith Qudsi – Sayings of Allah *Ta'ala* as revealed to the Prophet and related as *Hadith.*

Haajj – A Muslim who has performed Hajj.

Hajj – Obligatory pilgrimage to Makkah, the fifth tenet of Islam.

Hajj-e-badl – Performing hajj on behalf of someone else; hajj by proxy.

Halaal – Lawful, permissible (action/food etc).

Haraam – Unlawful, forbidden (action/food etc).

Haram – Sacred sanctuary of Makkah, Medinah and Masjid-e- Aqsa.

Hijaab – Headdress worn by a Muslim woman.

Hidaya – Guidance from Allah *Ta'ala*.

Hijrah – Migration, referring to the Islamic calendar.

Hilaal – Crescent, first-day (visible) moon in lunar month.

Ibadaat – Plural of *ibadah*, a comprehensive word for various kinds of worships.

Iftaar – Breaking fast at the end of day's fasting during the month of Ramadan.

Ihsan – Constantly perfecting oneself.

Ijtehad – Consent of the Ulema in the light of Islamic teachings.

Iman – Faith.

Imtihan – Test.

Insha Allah – "God willing", a frequently used term on the lips of a Muslim.

Istighfaar – Seeking the forgiveness of Allah (SWT).

Iqama – Call to prayer said at the beginning of the prayer.

Isha – Night prayer before bedtime, one of the five obligatory prayers.

Islam – The religion of the Muslims, a monotheistic faith regarded as revealed through Muhammad (PBUH) as the Prophet of Allah. It is an unconditional submission to the Will of Allah.

Iyadat-ul-mareed – Visiting the sick.

Jaiz – Permissible deed.

Janabah – A state of uncleanliness after seminal discharge.

Janaza – Islamic funeral.

Jannah – Paradise.

Jihad – (a) Striving to achieve patience, peace and piety as in Qur'an 22:78, 25:49-52 and 61:9-11; (b) Conditional fight if attacked; to fight against oppression, injustice or on breaking a treaty, as mentioned in Qur'an 2:190-193, 4:74-76, 9:29. The references here have to be read under their true historical and political contexts. Contrary to popular opinion, *jihad* is not "holy war." "Holy war" translates as *Harb al-muqaddas* in Arabic which is nowhere mentioned in the Qur'an or *Ahadith*.

Jinn – A creation of Allah made from fire, just like man was made from dust. Shaitan is amongst *jinn*. An imperceptible being not to be confused with genie or demon.

Jum'a – Friday. Obligatory Friday afternoon congregational prayer in lieu of *Zuhr*.

Ka'aba – The first masjid on earth, cubical in shape, built by Ibraheem (AS). It is situated in Makkah. Muslims around the world face Ka'aba for prayers.

Kafir – A non-believer in Allah.

Khilal – Flossing teeth. See *miswaak*.

Kibr – Arrogance.

Kosher – Meat of permissible animals slaughtered according to Jewish tradition. This food is permissible for Muslims if *halaal* is not available, but watch out for the wine!

Kuffara – Condoning of sin through a charity.

Maghrib – Evening prayer soon after sunset; one of the five obligatory prayers.

Masaah – Wiping head and (washing) feet during *wudu*.

Masjid – Mosque.

Mahram – Relationship of husband and wife is *mahram* to each other. Also, a relationship in which a man and a woman cannot marry, e.g., brother and sister.

Mazoor – Incapacitated or incapable.

Miswaak – Toothbrush made from tender root of a plant, *Salvadora persica*, recommended by Prophet Muhammad (PBUH). See *khilal*.

Momin – A Muslim.

Muharram – First month of the Islamic calendar, it is lunar.

Muslim – One who submits to the Will of Allah, peacefully and unconditionally; a follower of Islam.

Nafl salaat – Optional prayers for more virtues from Allah (SWT).

Najaz – Unclean.

Namaaz –Farsi (or Persian) word for prayer, *salaat*.

Ni'ma – Allah's favours and blessings.

Niyyah – Intention. *Niyyah* is essential for all kinds of *ibadaat*.

PBUH – "Peace be upon him," a *du'a* mentioned after the name of every prophet.

Qada – Belated action.

Qadr – Divine preordainment, Destiny.

Qibla – Direction of prayer in Islam, i.e., facing Ka'aba (in Makkah).

Qur'an – The Book revealed to Prophet Muhammad (PBUH) as a final guidance to humanity; last of the four Revealed Books including the Torah, Psalms and The Gospel. Unlike the other books, the Qur'an, which remains unchanged to this day, is considered by Muslims to be a lasting miracle.

RA – *"RadiAllahu anh /anha"* ("May Allah be pleased with him/her"). This *du'a* is said for the Companions of Prophet Muhammad (PBUH).

Rahma – Allah's mercy.

Rak'a – A unit of prayer; e.g., *fajr* prayer has two units; plural is *raka'tain, raka'a.*

Ramadan – Ninth month of the Islamic calendar.

Rasool Allah – (*Rasoolullah*) Messenger of Allah.

Rizq – Bounties of Allah (SWT).

Rukuu – A part of *salaat*.

Ruqa- – Plural of Ar-ruqyah.

Ruqyah – Qur'anic verses and the like recited to seek cure for sickness.

Sabr – Patience, endurance.

Sadaqa-e-jariah – Charity that brings everlasting rewards.

Sahaba – Companions of Prophet Muhammad (PBUH). *Sahabiaat* is the feminine gender.

Sajoodus-sahoo – This is *Sajda* performed when certain mistake is done during *salaat*.

Sahoo – Forgetting; a person is supposed to perform *Sajoodus-sahoo* if he forgets to perform an obligatory part of *salaat*.

Salaat/salaa/salaah/namaaz – Prayer; one of the five tenets of Islam. Muslims pray five times a day, a minimum of five minutes at a time, after *wudu*; *salawaat* is plural.

Salaatuz janaza – Islamic funeral prayer.

Saleh – The righteous ones; plural, *saleheen*.

Satr – The minimum clothing with which a Muslim is required to cover his body.

Sawm/siyam – Fasting; plural of fasting.

Shahada – Declaration of the second tenet of Islam: "There's no god but Allah, Muhammad (PBUH) is Allah's Messenger."

Shaitaan – One who shuns goodness and tempts to evil. Iblis was Shaitaan; an imperceptible being.

Shifa – A demonstration of healing; Islam approves seeking treatment for diseases from doctors, but *shifa* comes only from Allah.

Shukr – Giving thanks.

Siyam – (sing. *Sawm*) Fasting during the month of Ramadan. This is not just going hungry, but also to practise piety in all respects more seriously.

Sunnah – The sayings, deeds and acts of Prophet Muhammad (PBUH) and those approved by him. This is the second main source of Islamic authority after the Qur'an.

Surah – A chapter of the Qur'an; there are 114 *surahs* in the Qur'an.

SWT – "*Subhanahu wa Ta'ala*" ("Magnificent and Great"), said after the name of Allah.

Tafseer – Commentary (on the Qur'an).

Tahara – Personal cleanliness including wash after urinating or passing stool. This concept in Islam with reference to *ibadaat* has a deep significance. In addition to general cleanliness, it is purification following menstruation and childbirth confinement for women, and after seminal discharge or intercourse for men and women. A full body bath with the intention of purifying oneself following any of these acts is incumbent upon every Muslim before any prayers.

Tajweed – Special way to recite the Qur'an.

Takabbur – Egoism.

Taqwa – Piety, righteousness.

Taraweeh – Special prayers performed after *salatul-ish'a* every night during the month of Ramadan.

Taqwa – Perpetual awareness of Allah and reverence to Him.

Tasbeeh – Concurrent utterances of praise to Allah.

Tashahhud – Part of the recitation during *salaat*.

Tawakkul – Being satisfied for whatever Allah has bestowed.

Tawaf – Circumambulation of the Ka'aba.

Tayammum – Performing *wudu* without water, due to scarcity of water or in case
water is not to be poured on the body for medical reasons.

Ulema – Plural for *a'alim*, a person learned in the field of religion.

Ummah – Community of Muslims.

Umra – Lesser pilgrimage, *Hajjul-asghar*.

Wallahu A'lam – 'Allah (SWT) alone has the knowledge'.

Wasiyah – Last will (testament).

Wudu – Washing face, hands, wiping of head and (washing) of feet before prayers;
ablution.

Zabiha – See *dhabeha.*

Zakah – Obligatory charity (2.5% of the extra savings held over a period of one year)
given to the poor. *Zakah* is one of the five tenets of Islam.

Zakaat al-fitr – Another obligatory small charity (worth feeding one) given to the poor
by the fasting Muslims during the month of Ramadan.

Zawal – Time when the sun crosses the zenith.

Zikr – Remembrance /recitation of the attributes of Allah, or passages from Qur'an
and the like. This is done either silently or openly to gain virtues.

Zuhr – Mid-afternoon prayer, one of five obligatory prayers performed daily.

Two Poems

By Salimah Ribeiro-Dewji

A Prayer to Allah Subhanahu

Allah, hear the echoes in my heart,
as I sit alone at night
I hold my Tasbeeh close to me
hoping to see Your Light

Sometimes I cry, because I think I'm lost,
and my body is full of fear,
But then I hear that little whisper,
"Don't worry, I'm Here..."

Show me how to restore my sight
and to remember we are a team
Hold my hand through this darkness
onto Your Path of Sirat-ul-Mustaqeem

Let me smell the Roses from Your
Beautiful Garden,
and feel the soft breeze on my cheek,
every time I sit to meditate, this is all
I truly seek.

Only You can dry away my tears,
and make me smile for real
Only You can come to rescue me,
only You know how I feel...

Allah, hear the echoes in my heart,
As I sit alone at night
I hold my Tasbeeh close to me,
Hoping to see Your Light.

My Compass

Allah, my compass
give me direction
the location of my soul
that I may find my way home...

I've walked the streets of sadness
with tears filling the gutters

I've flown over miles of loneliness
and landed on fields of pain

I've swam across rivers of darkness
and been washed ashore islands of fear

O Allah my compass
give me direction
the location of my soul
that I may find my way home...

Salimah Ribeiro-Dewji of Toronto is a self-taught artist and poet. Her email address is spiritualartist@hotmail.com

ABOUT THE AUTHOR

BORN in Mysore, India, in 1936, Syed Rafeeq Muhammad Amjad is the son of Syed Abdul Rahim and Aamina Begum. His grandfather, Hazrath Syed Abdul Latheef, was from Baghdad, and served in the Imperial British Army in India as a Regimentdar (Commandant) in Mysore City.

Mr Syed has a degree in Agricultural Sciences and worked in various agricultural research programs in India before migrating to Canada in 1965. He studied Clinical Chemistry, worked at Sunnybrook Health Science Centre in Toronto, and, since his arrival, has been active in the affairs of Toronto's Muslim community.

He is married to Amthul Malik, B.A, B.Ed, daughter of the late Capt. Syed Abdul Kareem. They have two sons (Neman is an environmental engineer and computer consultant and Usman a product manager for a major software company) and a daughter (Safiya, who is a training specialist).

Both he and his wife Malika taught *Deeniyaat* (Islamic Studies) to children and adolescents at home and in the *masjid* (mosque) for several years. Upon his retirement from Sunnybrook in 1995, Mr Syed established and occasionally led *Salaathul Jum'a* at Clarkson Community Centre in Mississauga before the ISNA Canada Mosque was built in September 2000.

Mr and Mrs Syed have traveled in India, England, Canada, the United States, Saudi Arabia, Egypt, Turkey, Malaysia and Singapore. *Allah Ta'ala* accorded them the opportunity to perform Hajj in 1979 (1401 AH), 1987 and again in 2002 at the invitation of Muslim World League in Canada.

Upon retirement, Mr and Mrs Syed registered at four local hospitals as volunteers to visit Muslim patients, which they continue to do to this date. *Alhamdulillah*, Mr Syed was never sick or hospitalized, but has had many opportunities to observe and chat with patients and/or their care givers in hospitals for several years during routine patient visits.

Mr and Mrs Syed are Pastoral Care Visitors to Trillium Health Care Centre (Mississauga Hospital and Queensway General), Credit Valley Hospital in Mississauga, and Halton Healthcare Services in Oakville. Mr Syed is also a Muslim Pastoral Visitor to Sunnybrook and Women's College Health Science Centre in Toronto, and other geriatric care facilities of Mississauga. Presently, he is an executive member of two hospital advisory committees.

Mr Syed co-authored the *Multifaith Prayer/Meditation Book* published by The Credit Valley Hospital, as well as *Religious and Spiritual Beliefs and Practices in Health Care* published by Trillium Health Centre. To help patients who did not speak English, Mr Syed compiled a booklet of phrases commonly used by the medical staff and patients, which has been translated into 26 languages. Mr Syed was honoured with a special award for his work by the hospital.

Mr and Mrs Syed are coordinators of Muslim Support Services for the Sick and Elderly and involved in the orientation program for volunteers who visit the sick in hospitals. He is the founding Coordinator of the Patient Visitation Program at the headquarters of the Islamic Society of North America (Canada) in Mississauga, and addresses hospital staff, students and others about Islamic practices and the expectations of Muslim patients.

In 2002, Mr Syed received ISNA Canada's prestigious Community Service Award.

NOTES

NOTES

NOTES

NOTES

NOTES

NOTES

NOTES

NOTES